THE COMPLETE TEA RECIPE BOOK

Taste Various Blends of Easy, Amazing, Delicious, and Comforting Handmade Tea Recipes for Everyday

Emma E. Lester

TABLE OF CONTENT

INTRODUCTION

Welcome to the world of tea, a brew cherished for its flavour, aroma, and health advantages for many years. This cookbook is the ideal resource to delve into tea recipes, whether you're a tea connoisseur or brand-new to the beverage.

Tea is more than just a straightforward beverage; it's a skill that calls for expertise, attention, and patience. Each type of tea has a distinct flavour profile that can be complemented or increased by using different ingredients and methods. This handbook has some of the tastiest and most inventive tea recipes to delight your palate and show you new ways to enjoy tea.

You may find recipes for numerous types of tea in this cookbook, including black tea, green tea, white tea, herbal tea, and more. Along with tea-infused foods like tea cakes, tea-infused rice, and tea-smoked salmon, we have also included recipes for tea-based drinks like lattes, tea smoothies, and tea cocktails.

We consider tea more than just a beverage; it is a way of life. Whether it's a warm cup of tea in the morning to start your day, an iced tea to cool you off on a hot summer day, or a soothing cup of tea before bed, tea may be enjoyed at any time of the day.

The numerous health advantages of tea are also well-known. Antioxidants found in abundance in it may assist in preventing cell damage and lower the incidence of chronic illnesses. Caffeine, which is present in tea, can heighten physical and mental performance.

This cookbook is intended to pique your interest in tea and encourage you to learn new flavours, methods, and health advantages. So let's explore the amazing world of tea recipes together when the kettle is on, and you're enjoying a cup of tea.

1.CHAI TEA

cooking time

Prep:2 mins

Cook:5 mins

Ingredients

- 2 mugs milk (or use almond milk)
- 2 English Breakfast tea bags
- 6 cracked cardamom pods
- ½ cinnamon stick
- a grating of fresh nutmeg
- 2 cloves
- 2-4 tsp light brown soft sugar

Method

1. In a saucepan, warm the milk over a very low heat. After pouring the contents of the tea bags into the pan, add the cinnamon stick, nutmeg, cloves, and cardamom pods that have been cracked.
2. Add light brown soft sugar as need to sweeten (chai tea should be sweet, but you can use less if you choose), then let steep for 10 Mins without boiling. Drink after straining into cups of.

2.CHAI TEA MIX

Prep Time: 30 mins

Total Time: 30 mins

Servings: 36

Ingredients

- 2 ½ cups of white sugar
- 1 ½ cups of unsweetened instant tea
- 1 cup of nonfat dry milk powder
- 1 cup of powdered non-dairy creamer
- 1 cup of French vanilla flavored powdered non-dairy creamer
- 2 tsp ground ginger
- 2 tsp ground cinnamon
- 1 tsp ground cloves
- 1 tsp ground cardamom

Directions

1. In a sizable dish, mix the sugar, instant tea, milk powder, nondairy creamer, and vanilla-flavored creamer. Add the cardamom, ginger, cinnamon, and cloves. In a food processor or blender, blend 1 cup of at a time until a fine powder is obtained.
2. For 1 serving, mix 2 heaping tbsp of chai tea mix with boiling water.

3.CHANDRA CHAI MOON TEA RECIPE

Ingredients:

- 5 cups of water
- 1 tsp whole cloves
- 1/2 tsp fennel seeds
- 1/2 tsp licorice root
- 1/2 tsp whole allspice berries
- 1 vanilla bean
- 3 tbsp honey
- 2 % milk

Directions:

1. Water, cloves, fennel seeds, licorice root, allspice berries, and vanilla bean are mixd in a pot. For 40 to 50 Mins, cook the dish tightly covered at a low temperature. Add honey after filtering into an appropriate container. Add milk and taste.

4.CITRUS-HONEY GREEN TEA

Prep Time: 10 mins

Total Time: 10 mins

Servings: 1

Ingredients

- 1 (2 inch) piece lemon zest, slice into thin slivers
- 2 tsp boiling water
- 2 tsp green tea powder
- ¾ cup of hot water

- ½ cup of freshly squeezed grapefruit juice
- 3 tbsp freshly squeezed lemon juice
- 1 tsp honey

Directions

2. Lemon zest should be placed in a big cup of or mug. 2 tsp of boiling water should be added, covered, and steeped for about 3 Mins. Add boiling water and green tea powder after stirring. Juices from lemon, grapefruit, and honey should be added. Stir well, then plate.

5.COCOA TEA MIX RECIPE

Prep Time: 10 mins

Total Time: 10 mins

Servings: 1

Ingredients

- 1 ½ cups of boiling water
- 1 Earl Grey tea bag
- 3 tbsp milk
- 1 ½ tbsp hot cocoa mix
- 2 tsp white sugar

Directions

3. Place a tea bag in a mug of boiling water, and steep for 2 Mins. Add milk, hot cocoa mix, and sugar after removing the tea bag. Stir for 20 seconds or until thoroughly mixd.

6. EASY AUTHENTIC MASALA CHAI

Prep Time: 5 mins

Cooking Time: 16 mins

Total Time: 21 mins

Servings: 2

Ingredients

- 1 ½ cups of water
- 1 (1/2 inch) piece fresh ginger, chop up
- 4 whole cloves
- ½ cinnamon stick
- 5 pods green cardamom pods, crushed
- 1 pod black cardamom, split open
- 2 black tea bags
- ⅔ cup of milk
- 2 tbsp white sugar

Directions

4. In a small pot, bring water to a boil. Add the green and black cardamoms, ginger, cloves, cinnamon stick, and water. Simmer for 5 Mins to let the flavors blend. Add the tea bags, then simmer for one to two Mins. Bring back to a boil after adding milk and sugar. Pour the tea into the mugs.

7.EMERALD-DROP SNOW TEA

Prep Time: 10 mins

Cooking Time: 5 mins

Total Time: 15 mins

Servings: 2

Ingredients

- 3 cups of hot water
- 2 tbsp Italian red wine, or more as need
- 2 tbsp white sugar
- ¾ tsp ground cinnamon
- ¼ tsp ground nutmeg
- ¼ tsp ground ginger
- 4 fresh spearmint leaves
- 1 leaf fresh mint leaf
- ½ apple, cubed

Directions

5. Bring to a boil the following ingredients: water, red wine, sugar, cinnamon, nutmeg, ginger, spearmint leaves, and mint leaf. Add apple to the mixture after lowering the heat. For about five Mins, simmer tea until apple can be readily pierced with a fork. Tea should be poured into a mug after removing apple with a slotted spoon or strainer.

8.FUSS FREE HOT CRANBERRY TEA

Prep Time: 5 mins

Cooking Time: 10 mins

Total Time: 15 mins

Servings: 26

Ingredients

- ½ gallon orange juice
- 1 (64 fluid ounce) bottle cranberry-raspberry juice
- 1 (16 ounce) can pineapple juice
- 2.25 ounce small red cinnamon candies
- ½ gallon water
- 8 tea bags

Directions

6. In a sizable stockpot, mix the orange juice, cranberry-raspberry juice, pineapple juice, and cinnamon candies. Cook over high heat until the candies melt.
7. Pouring the water and tea bags into the juice mixture after boiling the mixture of water and tea bags in a separate pot for 5 to 10 Mins. Serve warm.

9.HONEY GINGER CLEANSING DETOX TEA

INGREDIENTS

- 1 knob (1-inch) ginger
- 1 tbsp honey
- 2 limes: one for the juice, one for the slices

DIRECTIONS

1. Wash lime and slice in half. Squeeze and collect the juice. Peel and grate the ginger.
2. Boil 2 cups of water and pour into a tea kettle. Add lime juice, lime wedges, honey, and grated ginger.
3. Infuse for 5 Mins and serve, garnished with lime wedges.

10.GINGER-TURMERIC HERBAL TEA

Prep Time: 5 mins

Cooking Time: 15 mins

Total Time: 20 mins

Servings: 2

Ingredients

- 2 cups of water
- ½ tsp ground turmeric
- ½ tsp chop up fresh ginger

- ½ tsp ground cinnamon
- 1 tbsp honey
- 1 lemon wedge

Directions

1. Add turmeric, ginger, and cinnamon to a small pot of boiling water. Medium-low heat should be used to simmer for 10 Mins.
2. Tea should be strained into a tall glass; add honey and a wedge of lemon before serving.

11.HONEY CHAI LATTE

Ingredients:

- 16 Whole All-Spice Berries
- 16 Whole Cardamom Pods or ½ tsp of Ground Cardamom
- 6 Whole Black Peppercorns
- 2 Cinnamon Sticks, 2 inches long
- 1 Slice (1/4-inch) Fresh Ginger or 1 tsp Ground Ginger
- 2 ½ Cups of Water
- 2 tsp Darjeeling or Other Black Tea Leaves
- ½ Cup of Queen Honey North Dakota Sweet Clover Honey
- 2 Cups of Low-Fat Mild, Hot

Directions:

1. Whole spices can be coarsely ground individually in a mortar and pestle or collectively in an electric grinder.
2. Mix water, ginger, and ground spices in a medium pot.

3. Boiling, then turning down the heat and simmering for 25 Mins
4. Add loose tea leaves and boil for an additional three Mins (longer simmering will make the concentrate bitter)
5. Remove from heat, pour through cheesecloth or a fine-mesh strainer into a medium basin, then mix in the honey to dissolve.
6. Put off serving till later.
7. Stir the chai concentrate into the heated milk and serve right away.

12.HOT AND SPICY HIMALAYAN TEA (CHAI TEA)

Prep Time: 5 mins

Cooking Time: 25 mins

Additional Time: 10 mins

Total Time: 40 mins

Servings: 6

Ingredients

- 7 cups of water
- 6 tbsp light brown sugar
- 1 ¼ inch piece fresh ginger root, peel off and chop up
- 1 cinnamon stick
- 6 green cardamom pods
- 12 whole cloves
- 2 bay leaves
- 1 tbsp fennel seeds
- ½ tsp black peppercorns
- 2 tbsp Darjeeling tea leaves
- 1 cup of milk

Directions

1. In a pot, mix the following ingredients: water, brown sugar, ginger root, cinnamon stick, cardamom pods, cloves, bay leaves, fennel seeds, and peppercorns. Cover the pot and bring the ingredients to a boil for 20 Mins. Tea leaves should be added to the pot after it has been taken off the heat. Tea is strained into tea cups of after being mixd with milk and brought to a boil.
2. Cook's Note: If you like, you can replace the fennel seeds with anise seeds. If preferred, swap the brown sugar for honey.

13.HOT CHAI LATTE

Prep Time: 5 mins

Cooking Time: 10 mins

Total Time: 15 mins

Servings: 2

Ingredients

- 1 cup of milk
- 1 cup of water
- 1 large strip of orange peel
- 3 whole cloves
- 1 (3 inch) cinnamon stick
- 3 whole black peppercorns
- 1 pinch ground nutmeg
- 4 tsp white sugar
- 2 tsp black tea leaves

Directions

1. Over medium-high heat, mix the milk and water in a saucepan. Add the orange peel, cloves, cinnamon stick, peppercorns, nutmeg, sugar, and tea leaves to the pan after the mixture has warmed. Bring to a boil, then lower the heat to medium-low, cover, and simmer for however long you'd like. Pour into mugs after straining away the spices.

14. HOT SPICED TEA FOR THE HOLIDAYS

Prep Time: 5 mins

Cooking Time: 10 mins

Additional Time: 5 mins

Total Time: 20 mins

Servings: 6

Ingredients

- 6 cups of water
- 1 tsp whole cloves
- 1 (1 inch) piece cinnamon stick
- 6 tea bags (such as Lipton®)
- ¾ cup of orange juice
- ½ cup of white sugar
- ¼ cup of pineapple juice
- 2 tbsp lemon juice

Directions

2. Add cinnamon stick and cloves to a saucepan of water. Boiling water should then be turned off the heat. Tea bags should be added to the water and let to steep for at least five Mins, or until the desired strength is reveryed. Take out and throw away the tea bags, cinnamon stick, and cloves.

3. In a saucepan, mix orange juice, sugar, pineapple juice, and lemon juice; bring to a boil. Cooking and stirring the juice mixture is required to completely dissolve the sugar. Serve hot tea that has been flavored with the juice mixture.

15.CHAI HOT CHOCOLATE

Prep Time5 Mins

Cooking Time10 Mins

Total Time15 Mins

INGREDIENTS

- 1/2 cup of water
- 2 tbsp Dutch-processed unsweetened cocoa powder
- 1 tbsp sugar (non-compulsory)
- 2 whole cloves, crushed
- 1/2 tsp ground cardamom (cardamom powder)
- 1/2 tsp ground cinnamon (cinnamon powder)
- 1/4 tsp ground ginger
- 2 cups of milk
- 125 g milk / dark chocolate

INSTRUCTIONS

1. In a pan over medium-high heat, add water. Add cocoa powder gradually while stirring continually to prevent lumps from forming when the water is lukewarm. Stir in the sugar (if using), then add.

2. Continuously stir. Add cinnamon, ginger, cloves, and cardamom. Stir and fully heat for about three Mins. The mixture must come to a boil. Fill with milk. include chocolate Mix the chocolate until it melts. To every serving cup of, divide.
3. Add whipped cream, marshmallows, cocoa powder, or chocolate syrup as a garnish.

16.LAVENDER MINT TEA

Prep/Total Time: 15 min.

Ingredients

- 1/4 cup of thinly split fresh mint leaves
- 4 tsp dried lavender flowers
- 1/2 tsp chop up fresh rosemary
- 4 cups of boiling water
- 2 tsp honey, non-compulsory

Directions

1. Mix the mint, lavender, and rosemary in a big basin. Add some hot water. For 4 Mins, cover and steep. Remove mint combination from tea and discard. If using honey, stir it in. Serve right away.

17. LEMON VERBENA MINT DETOX TEA

Prep Time: 5 mins

Cooking Time: 3 mins

Total Time: 8 mins

Servings: 1

Ingredients

- 1 cup of boiling water
- 1 sprig fresh lemon verbena (about 10 leaves)
- 1 sprig fresh mint (about 15 leaves)
- 1 tsp honey, or as need

Directions

2. Pour boiling water over the verbena and mint sprigs; steep for 3 to 4 Mins, or until desired flavor is achieved. Add honey and mix.
3. Cook's Notes: I leave the leaves attached to the stem so I can simply remove them just before serving; no straining is required.

18. DAIRY-FREE COCONUT DIRTY CHAI LATTE FOR TWO

Prep Time: 10 mins

Cooking Time: 5 mins

Total Time: 15 mins

Servings: 2

Ingredients

- 1 cup of brewed chai tea
- 1 cup of warm coconut milk
- 1 tsp instant espresso powder
- ½ tsp ground cinnamon
- 1 tsp honey
- 1 tbsp unsweetened shredded coconut

Directions

1. Blend the following ingredients in a blender: chai tea, coconut milk, espresso powder, and cinnamon. Stir into 2 mugs, top with honey, then top with coconut flakes.

19.EASY MASALA CHAI (TEA) RECIPE – SPICED CHAI

Cooking Time: 20 MINS

total time: 20 MINS

INGREDIENTS

- 2 1/4 cups of (532 ml) filtered water
- 1 3-inch cinnamon stick, ceylon or cassia are both fine
- 3 whole cloves
- 4 green cardamom pods, cracked open and deseeded (I throw seeds & pods in)
- 3 black peppercorns
- 1/2 tsp fennel seeds, non-compulsory
- 1/2- inch (~4 g) fresh ginger, peel off and thinly split
- 3 black tea bags or sub 3 tsp loose leaf black tea, depending on brand, tea bags/leaves vary in strength (See Note 1)
- 1 cup of (8 oz) whole milk, or 2% reduced fat milk
- 4 tsp (20 g) turbinado cane sugar, or raw cane sugar

INSTRUCTIONS

2. A medium saucepan is heated on high. Add the water, ginger, fennel seeds (if used), cardamom pods, cloves, cinnamon stick, and black peppercorns. Observe Note 2 Add the tea bags or leaves once it has reveryed a boil.
3. Depending on how strong you want the tea and spices, reduce the heat to medium-low and simmer gently for 7–10 Mins. It will dim somewhat and change hue to a deep burgundy.
4. Stir in the milk and sugar. Put the heat on high (or allow the milk to come to a boil on its own, as I do on any given day). For a further five Mins, lower the heat to medium.

5. Depending on how "cooked" you prefer your milk, turn the heat up to high and let it come to a rolling boil for 1–2 Mins when you're ready to serve. (See Notation 3) If you'd want to enhance the flavor and make the chai creamier, aerate it with a ladle.
6. Pour through a strainer into cups of and, if desired, add extra sweetness.

20.PERFECT VANILLA TEA

Prep Time: 5 mins

Total Time: 5 mins

Servings: 1

Ingredients

- 1 cup of boiling water
- 1 orange pekoe tea bag
- 2 tbsp milk
- 1 tsp white sugar
- ½ tsp vanilla extract
- ½ tsp ground cinnamon

Directions

1. Fill a mug with hot water. After three Mins, extract and discard the tea bag from the water.
2. Tea should be blended with milk, sugar, cinnamon, and vanilla essence.

21.RAILROAD-STYLE CHAI

Prep Time: 5 mins

Cooking Time: 5 mins

Total Time: 10 mins

Servings: 4

Ingredients

- 2 cups of water
- 1 tbsp fennel seed
- 4 whole cloves, or more as need
- 1 ½ tsp cardamom seeds
- 2 cups of whole milk
- 4 black tea bags, or more as need
- 1 tbsp white sugar, or as need

Directions

1. In a saucepan, bring water to a boil before adding the cardamom, fennel, and cloves. Continue to boil the water for three more Mins.
2. Tea bags are added, heat is reduced to low, and the liquid is boiled for 2 to 3 Mins, or until the tea has a strong flavor without being bitter. The process is repeated after stirring in the milk.
3. Tea should be strained into four tea glasses; add sugar as need.

Cook's Notes:

It is crucial to utilize a low-cost granulated tea. I tried making this for years using the best Darjeeling and Asaam teas I could get, but it never turned out properly. The secret is the cheap powdered tea, which is essentially what we put in tea bags. Strong-flavored tea is necessary to counter the flavor that the spices add.

22.ROEBUCK'S RUSSIAN TEA

Prep Time: 10 mins

Cooking Time: 30 mins

Total Time: 40 mins

Servings: 20

Ingredients

- 1 gallon water
- 3 cups of white sugar
- 16 whole cloves
- 16 whole allspice berries
- 4 tea bags
- 1 (46 fluid ounce) can pineapple juice
- 6 lemons, juiced
- 4 oranges, juiced

Directions

1. Bring to a boil in a big pot the following ingredients: water, sugar, cloves, and allspice berries. Simmer the heat down. Tea bags are added, steeped for 5 Mins, and then left in the pot. Orange juice, lemon juice, and pineapple juice should be added. Simmer for a further 15 Mins or until well heated. If preferred, take out the tea bags and spices.

23.RUSSIAN TEA

Prep Time: 10 mins

Total Time: 10 mins

Servings: 40

Ingredients

- 2 cups of white sugar
- 2 cups of orange-flavored drink mix (e.g. Tang)
- 1 cup of instant tea powder
- 1 (3 ounce) package powdered lemonade mix
- 2 tsp ground cinnamon
- ½ tsp ground cloves

Directions

2. In a sizable bowl, mix sugar, orange drink mix, tea powder, lemonade powder, ground cinnamon, and ground cloves; stir well. Keep in a container with a tight lid.
3. To provide: 1 cup of hot or cold water should be added to 3 to 4 tbsp of dry mix.

INGREDIENTS

- 2large tea bags, steeped (family size or several smaller tea bags)
- 0.5(46 ounce) can pineapple juice
- 1(6 ounce) can refrigerate orange juice, thawed
- 4tbsp lemon juice
- 1 1/2cups of sugar
- 1tsp ground cinnamon
- 1tsp ground cloves

DIRECTIONS

1. Steep tea, remove tea bags, whisk in sugar until it dissolves, then stir in other ingredients and refrigerate

25. SLOW COOKER CHAI

Prep Time: 15 mins

Cooking Time: 8 hrs

Additional Time: 5 mins

Total Time: 8 hrs 20 mins

Servings: 16

Ingredients

- 3 ½ quarts water
- 3 cinnamon sticks
- 15 green cardamom pods, split open and seeded
- 15 slices fresh ginger, peel off
- 25 whole cloves
- 3 whole black peppercorns
- 8 black tea bags
- 1 (14 ounce) can sweetened condensed milk

Directions

2. In a slow cooker, mix water, cinnamon sticks, cardamom pods, ginger, cloves, and peppercorns. 8 hours on high for cooking.
3. In the slow cooker, put tea bags, and let them brew for five Mins.
4. Condensed milk is added after the liquid has been strained into a clean container. Serve warm.

26.SPICED TEA MIX

Prep/Total Time: 10 min.

Ingredients

- 1 jar (21.1 ounces) orange breakfast drink mix
- 1 jar (6 ounces) sugar-free instant lemon iced tea mix
- 2/3 cup of sweetened lemonade drink mix
- 2 tsp ground cinnamon
- 1 tsp ground cloves
- additional ingredients for hot spiced tea:
- 1 cup of boiling water
- additional ingredients for hot spiced punch:
- 2 quarts apple juice or cider
- 1-1/2 cups of cranberry juice
- 3 cinnamon sticks (3-1/2 inches)

Directions

1. The first five ingredients should be mixd in an airtight container. For up to 6 months, store in a cool, dry location. Total yield: around 7-1/2 cups of.
2. Tea preparation: Stir well as you dissolve roughly 1 tbsp of tea mix in the boiling water. Produce: 1 serving.
3. Punch can be made by combining the liquids, 1/4 to 1/3 cup of tea mix, and cinnamon sticks in a 3-qt slow cooker. For four hours, cook on low with a cover. Around 12 servings per batch (6 ounces every).

27. TART ROSE AND GINGER TEA

Ingredients

- 1 ½ cups of boiling water
- 6 slices fresh ginger root
- 2 tbsp fresh rose petals, white base trimmed off
- ¼ lemon, juiced
- 3 tsp honey, or more as need
- 2 tbsp tart unsweetened cherry juice

Directions

1. In a small saucepan, bring water to a boil. Remove from heat. In a tea ball, mix ginger and rose petals. Steep for 6 Mins in boiling water.
2. Fill a cup of with lemon juice. Add honey and sour cherry juice and stir. Over top, pour ginger-rose tea.

28. TURMERIC COFFEE LATTE

Prep Time: 5 mins

Cooking Time: 5 mins

Total Time: 10 mins

Servings: 2

Ingredients

- 1 cup of coconut milk
- 1 tsp vanilla extract
- 2 packets stevia sweetener (such as Truvia®)
- ½ tsp ground turmeric
- ¼ tsp ground ginger
- ¼ tsp ground cinnamon
- 1 fluid ounce brewed espresso

Directions

1. In a saucepan, mix the coconut milk, cinnamon, ginger, turmeric, and stevia sweetener. Around 5 Mins of warming on medium heat.
2. Take the pot from the heat. Using an immersion blender, blend until foamy.
3. To serve, pour espresso into a mug. Add some frothed milk mixture on top.

29.ULTIMATE COLD RELIEF HOME REMEDY TEA

Prep Time: 10 mins

Total Time: 10 mins

Servings: 1

Ingredients

- 8 ounces water, or as needed
- 1 tbsp apple cider vinegar
- 1 tbsp honey
- 1 cinnamon stick

- 1 clove garlic, peel off and smashed

Directions

1. In a small saucepan, mix the water, vinegar, honey, cinnamon stick, and garlic. Heat to 100°F (38°C); then turn off the heat and pour into a mug.

30. WARM LEMON, HONEY, AND GINGER SOOTHER

Prep Time: 5 mins

Additional Time: 5 mins

Total Time: 10 mins

Servings: 4

Ingredients

- ¼ cup of honey, or as need
- 1 lemon, juiced
- 1 tbsp lightly grated ginger root
- ¼ tsp ground cinnamon
- 3 ½ cups of boiling water

Directions

2. In a teapot or 4-cup of glass measuring beaker with a spout, mix the honey, lemon juice, ginger, and cinnamon. Over the mixture, pour boiling water and whisk until the honey is dissolved.
3. For five Mins, cover the teapot and let it steep. Although it can be strained as the liquid is poured into a mug, the ginger should drop to the bottom.

31.ALMOND TEA

Prep Time: 5 mins

Total Time: c5 mins

Servings: 16

Ingredients

- 1 cup of white sugar
- 3 tbsp instant iced tea powder
- 2 cups of boiling water
- 1 (12 ounce) can refrigerate lemonade concentrate
- 2 tsp vanilla extract
- 1 tbsp almond extract
- 3 quarts cold water, or as needed

Directions

1. In a gallon container, mix sugar and instant tea powder. Lemonade concentrate and boiling water should be mixed well. Add almond and vanilla extracts after stirring, and then pour cold water into the container. To blend, stir.
2. Serve chilled or over ice when ready to serve.

32. BLACK TEA LEMONADE

Prep Time: 5 mins

Cooking Time: 5 mins

Additional Time: 2 hrs

Total Time: 2 hrs 10 mins

Servings: 8

Ingredients

- 5 cups of water
- ½ cup of white sugar
- 3 orange pekoe tea bags
- 1 (12 ounce) can refrigerate lemonade concentrate
- 5 cups of water

Directions

1. In a pot, heat 5 cups of water, the sugar, and when the mixture is boiling, add the tea bags. While you mix the remaining water with the lemonade concentrate in a big pitcher, let the tea steep. Discard the tea bags and pour the tea mixture into the lemonade. Before serving, stir and chill in the refrigerator.

33.BOBA

Prep Time: 10 mins

Cooking Time: 55 mins

Additional Time: 1 hrs 5 mins

Total Time: 2 hrs 10 mins

Servings: 5

Ingredients

- Tapioca Pearls:
- 7 cups of cold water
- ½ (8.8 ounce) package tapioca starch balls
- ½ cup of brown sugar
- ½ cup of white sugar
- Tea:
- 4 cups of brewed black tea (such as Lipton®), chilled
- 1 (14 ounce) can coconut cream
- 12 ice cubes
- 1 cup of milk
- ⅔ cup of white sugar

Directions

2. In a big stockpot, bring water to a boil. Tapioca should be added and simmered for 25 Mins. To avoid sticking, stir every so while. Remove from heat and let balls soak for 25 Mins in water.
3. Reset the heat on the stockpot, and simmer and stir for a further 25 Mins. Remove from heat and allow to rest for an additional 25 Mins or until the centers of the balls are no longer powder. Drain.

4. In a sizable basin, mix brown sugar and white sugar. Tapioca balls should be added to the sugar mixture. While making the tea, cover with a moist cloth and allow to rest for 15 Mins.
5. In a blender, mix the tea, coconut cream, ice, milk, and sugar until well-mixd.
6. Pour tea into every tall glass after adding 1/4 cup of tapioca. Use spoons or a big straw to suck up the tapioca as you enjoy it.

34.BOSTON ICED TEA

Prep Time: 20 mins

Cooking Time: 15 mins

Total Time: 35 mins

Servings: 14

Ingredients

- 1 gallon water
- 1 cup of white sugar
- 15 tea bags
- 1 (12 fluid ounce) can refrigerate cranberry juice concentrate

Directions

1. Large pot with water in it should be heated to boiling on high. Stir in the sugar until it is dissolved. Teabags should be added and steeped until the required strength is achieved. After adding the cranberry juice concentrate, let the mixture cool.

35.CARIBBEAN SORREL TEA

Prep Time: 5 mins

Cooking Time: 5 mins

Additional Time: 8 hrs

Total Time: 8 hrs 10 mins

Servings: 4

Ingredients

- 9 ounces dried red sorrel buds
- 3 tsp grated ginger
- 3 strips dried orange zest
- 1 white clove
- 1 quart water
- ⅔ cup of white sugar
- ice cubes

Directions

2. In a bowl, mix the sorrel, ginger, dried orange zest, and clove.
3. In a pot or kettle, bring water to a boil. Pour over the sorrel mixture. Add sugar and mix until it dissolves. Let mixture to steep for 8 hours to overnight at room temperature.
4. Pour sorrel mixture into a pitcher after passing it through a fine-mesh sieve; discard sediments. Serve chilled.

36.CHAI TEA LATTE

Prep Time: 5 mins

Total Time: 5 mins

Servings: 1

Ingredients

- ¾ cup of boiling water
- 1 chai tea bag
- 1 ½ tsp honey
- 1 tsp white sugar
- ¾ cup of milk

Directions

1. Place a chai tea bag in a mug, add boiling water, and steep for 4 to 6 Mins. Tea bag removed and thrown away.
2. To dissolve, stir sugar and honey into tea. For serving, add milk to the tea.

37.CHERRY GINGER INFUSED TEA

Prep Time: 10 mins

Cooking Time: 5 mins

Additional Time: 2 hrs

Total Time: 2 hrs 15 mins

Servings: 4

Ingredients

- 1 cup of pitted cherries
- 1 (2 inch) piece fresh ginger, peel off and split
- 3 tbsp white sugar
- 4 cups of filtered water, separated
- 4 (2 g) bags green tea
- 4 lemon slices
- 1 tbsp lemon juice, or as need

Directions

1. In a glass bowl, mix the cherries and the ginger pieces. Add 2 cups of filtered water to the cherry mixture after adding sugar.
2. Refrigerate bowl for two hours to overnight after covering with plastic wrap.
3. Pour 2 cups of nearly-boiling filtered water over the tea bags in a pitcher. tea for 90 seconds to steep. Discard tea bags after squeezing them into the pitcher.
4. Squeeze out extra liquid before pouring cherry-ginger water into a pitcher with green tea. Lemon juice and lemon slices should be served.
5. Editor's note: The cherries and ginger are fully accounted for in the nutritional information for this dish. The precise number of calories consumed will differ.

38.COOL RHUBARB ICED TEA

Prep Time: 15 mins

Cooking Time: 4 hrs

Additional Time: 8 hrs

Total Time: 12 hrs 15 mins

Servings: 24

Ingredients

- 10 stalks fresh rhubarb, chop up
- 2 cups of white sugar, or as need
- 1 quart water
- 1 quart water
- 8 black tea bags
- 1 tbsp honey
- 1 cup of white sugar

Directions

1. Put the rhubarb, sugar, and 1 quart of water in a big pot. After the rhubarb turns into a thick paste, simmer for about 4 hours on low heat, stirring occasionally to prevent burning. After cooling, spoon mixture into ice cube trays, and freeze for one night.
2. 1 quart of water should come to a boil. Pour over the tea bags in a pitcher. Add sugar and honey and stir. Cool, then chill in the refrigerator. With rhubarb ice cubes, serve chilled iced tea.

39.CRANBERRY ORANGE ICED TEA

Servings: 6

Ingredients

- 2 cups of boiling water
- 6 cranberry herb tea bags
- ¼ cup of lemon juice
- 9 packets Sweet'N Low granulated sugar substitute
- 2 ½ cups of cold water
- 1 ½ cups of orange juice

Directions

1. Pour the boiling water over the tea bags in a big pitcher. After 5 Mins of steeping, remove and discard the tea bags.
2. Lemon juice and Sweet'N Low are added; stir until Sweet'N Low dissolves. Orange juice and cold water should be mixd.
3. Keep in the refrigerator until very cold.
4. Pour into large glasses with ice.

40. DELICIOUS MATCHA GREEN TEA FRAPPUCCINO

Prep Time: 5 mins

Total Time: 5 mins

Servings: 1

Ingredients

- 2 cups of ice cubes
- 1 ½ cups of milk
- 1 fluid ounce vanilla-flavored syrup (such as Torani®), or as need
- 1 ½ tsp green tea powder (matcha)

Directions

1. Ice, milk, vanilla syrup, and green tea powder are all blended in a blender until they are completely smooth.

41. DELIGHTFUL PUNCH

Prep Time: 20 mins

Total Time: 20 mins

Servings: 12

Ingredients

- 1 cup of strong brewed black tea
- 1 cup of grapefruit juice
- 1 cup of orange juice
- ½ cup of pineapple juice
- ½ cup of simple syrup
- 1 liter ginger ale soda

Directions

2. Tea, pineapple juice, orange juice, grapefruit juice, and simple syrup should all be mixd in a sizable punch bowl. Add the ginger ale and then serve.

42. FRESH CRANBERRY SPICED TEA

Prep Time: 10 mins

Cooking Time: 30 mins

Additional Time: 8 hrs

Total Time: 8 hrs 40 mins

Servings: 16

Ingredients

- 1 pound fresh or refrigerate cranberries
- 3 quarts cold water
- 2 cups of orange juice
- 2 ⅛ cups of pineapple juice
- ¼ cup of lemon juice
- 2 cups of white sugar, or as need
- 1 (3 inch) cinnamon stick
- 1 tsp whole cloves
- ½ tsp whole allspice berries

Directions

3. In a big pot, mix the cranberries and water. Just until the berries pop, which takes about 5 Mins, bring to a boil. Remove from the heat and allow it cool for several hours at room temperature.
4. Remove the cranberries, then whisk in the sugar, orange juice, pineapple juice, lemon juice, and pineapple juice. Add the whole cloves, cinnamon stick, and allspice berries. a low boil is reveryed. Although it is already prepared to be served, leaving it to sit for the night will improve it even more.

43. FRIENDSHIP TEA

Prep Time: 10 mins

Total Time: 10 mins

Servings: 40

Ingredients

- ½ cup of instant tea powder
- 1 cup of sweetened lemonade powder
- 1 cup of orange-flavored drink mix (e.g. Tang)
- 1 tsp ground cinnamon
- ½ tsp ground cloves

Directions

1. Mix instant tea, lemonade powder, orange drink mix, cinnamon, and clove in a sizable basin. Mix thoroughly and keep in an airtight container.
2. Place 2 to 3 tsp of the mixture in a mug to serve. 1 cup of hot water is stirred in. As need, adjust.

44.GOOD OL' ALABAMA SWEET TEA

Prep Time: 1 mins

Cooking Time: 10 mins

Total Time: 11 mins

Servings: 16

Ingredients

- 2 cups of sugar
- ½ gallon water
- 1 tray ice cubes
- 3 family sized teabags of orange pekoe tea
- 3 cups of cold water, or as needed

Directions

1. Into a big pitcher, pour the sugar. In a big pan, bring water to a rolling boil. Remove from the heat when the water starts to boil, then add the teabags. Steep for five to six Mins.
2. Take out the tea bags and reheat the tea. Once it has barely begun to boil, pour it into the pitcher and stir until the sugar has completely dissolved. Half-fill the pitcher with ice, then stir until the majority of it melts. After that, add cold water to the pitcher's remaining capacity and whisk to mix.

45. GRANDMA'S RUSSIAN TEA

Prep Time: 5 mins

Cooking Time: 15 mins

Total Time: 20 mins

Servings: 12

Ingredients

- 2 family-sized tea bags
- 1 quart boiling water
- 1 ½ quarts water
- 1 cinnamon stick
- 6 whole cloves
- 1 (12 ounce) can pineapple juice
- 1 cup of white sugar
- 1 (6 ounce) can refrigerate orange juice concentrate
- 1 (6 ounce) can refrigerate lemonade concentrate
- 1 tsp ground allspice

Directions

1. Tea bags should be steeped in boiling water for 4 to 5 Mins, depending on desired strength. Take out and throw away the tea bags.
2. Bring 1 1/2 quarts of water, a cinnamon stick, and some cloves to a boil in a big pot.
3. To the boiling water, add the brewed tea, pineapple juice, sugar, orange juice and lemonade concentrates, allspice, and stir until the sugar is dissolved.
4. Serve right away, or turn down the heat and simmer until you're ready to serve.

46. GREEN TEA BERRY DELIGHT

Prep Time: 5 mins

Total Time: 5 mins

Servings: 1

Ingredients

- ½ cup of refrigerate blueberries
- 4 refrigerate strawberries
- 2 cups of iced green tea

Directions

1. At the bottom of a tall glass, add the blueberries and strawberries. Over the berries, pour the green tea.

47. HAWAIIAN PLANTATION ICED TEA

INGREDIENTS

- 1quart boiling water (make sure it is only barely boiling)
- 4orange pekoe tea bags
- 1quart ice cold water
- 1(16 ounce) can pineapple juice
- 1/2cup of simple syrup (non-compulsory)
- 1fresh pineapple, peel off, cored, and slice into spears

DIRECTIONS

2. Add the tea bags to the nearly boiling hot water in a big pitcher. For 2 to 4 Mins, steep the tea.
3. After removing the tea bags, add the ice water.
4. The pineapple juice should be added.
5. For about 1 1/2 hours, refrigerate until well cooled.
6. Serve the tea with pineapple spears as a garnish after pouring it over ice.

48.HOMEMADE PEVERY TEA

Prep Time: 5 mins

Cooking Time: 10 mins

Additional Time: 35 mins

Total Time: 50 mins

Servings: 6

Ingredients

- Pevery Syrup:
- 1 cup of water
- 1 cup of white sugar
- 2 slices fresh pevery, or more as need
- Tea:
- 6 cups of water
- 3 tea bags

Directions

1. In a saucepan, mix 1 cup of water, sugar, and pevery slices; bring to a boil. Lower heat to medium and simmer for about 5 Mins, breaking up pevery slices as you stir. After taking the pot off the heat, cover it and let the peveryes steep in the syrup for about 30 Mins. To remove the pevery slices, strain.
2. In a another saucepan, heat the remaining 6 cups of water to a boil. Take the pot off the heat, add the tea bags, cover it, and steep for about five Mins.
3. Take out the tea bags, add the pevery syrup, and let the tea come to room temperature. Keep chilled until you're ready to serve.

49.HONEY LEMON TEA

Prep Time: 5 mins

Cooking Time: 5 mins

Total Time: 10 mins

Servings: 1

Ingredients

- 1 cup of water
- 2 tsp honey
- 1 tsp fresh lemon juice
- 1 tsp white sugar, or as need

Directions

1. Put some water in the mug. Microwave for 1 minute 30 seconds with honey added.
2. Lemon juice should be added and mixed until honey is dissolved. Add sugar and mix.

50.HONEY MILK TEA - HONG KONG STYLE

Prep Time: 5 mins

Additional Time: 10 mins

Total Time: 15 mins

Servings: 1

Ingredients

- 2 orange pekoe tea bags
- 1 cup of boiling water
- 5 ice cubes
- 4 tsp sweetened condensed milk
- 3 tsp honey

Directions

1. Tea bags should be steeped in boiling water for 3 to 5 Mins, or until the color turns dark red. After letting the tea cool, throw away the tea bags.
2. In a glass or cocktail shaker, mix the honey, sweetened condensed milk, and ice cubes. Add the tea and well mix. (The ice may melt if the tea is still warm; you can add extra ice if you like.) You can now savor a potent, tasty milk tea.

51.ICED TEA RECIPE (EXTRA EASY)

Ingredients

- 8 cups of water, separated
- 6 bags black tea
- 1/3 cup of sugar, non-compulsory, adjust as need

Instructions

1. Bring half of the water to a boil in a saucepan. Add tea bags after removing from the heat. Ten Mins should be given to the tea bags to steep.
2. Tea bags should be taken out of the water. Reminder: Add sugar or your favourite sweetener to the tea while it's still boiling and stir until it dissolves if you want sweet tea.
3. To the tea, add the remaining water. Keep it in the fridge until it's completely cold (about an hour).
4. If preferred, garnish with ice, lemon slices, and fresh mint.

52.ICED TEA II

Prep Time: 10 mins

Cooking Time: 1 hrs

Total Time: 1 hrs 10 mins

Servings: 8

Ingredients

- 8 cups of water
- 3 orange pekoe tea bags
- ¾ cup of white sugar
- ½ cup of lemon juice

Directions

1. Bring water to a quick boil in a big pot. Drop the tea bags in after removing from the heat. For one hour, cover and let soak.
2. Mix the sugar and steeped tea in a big pitcher. Lemon juice should be added after the sugar has completely dissolved. Keep cold in the refrigerator.

53.KARKADEH (EGYPTIAN HIBISCUS ICED TEA)

Prep Time: 5 mins

Additional Time: 4 hrs

Total Time: 4 hrs 5 mins

Servings: 6

Ingredients

- ¼ cup of dried hibiscus petals
- 1 ½ quarts boiling water
- 2 tbsp white sugar, or more as need

Directions

1. Hibiscus flowers should be put in a pot with boiling water covering them. Add sugar as need, then let cool. Pour into a pitcher after straining. Keep in the refrigerator until very cold.

54. KUWAITI TRADITIONAL TEA

Prep Time: 2 mins

Cooking Time: 8 mins

Total Time: 10 mins

Servings: 1

Ingredients

- 1 ½ cups of water
- 2 whole cardamom pods, broken
- 1 pinch saffron powder
- 2 tea bags
- 1 tsp white sugar

Directions

2. Over medium heat, mix the water, saffron, and cardamom. Bring to a boil while covered. If you prefer stronger tea, steep the tea for an additional minute after adding the tea bags. Pour through a strainer into a cup of, and if desired, add sugar as need.

55.LEMON ALMOND TEA

Prep Time: 15 mins

Cooking Time: 15 mins

Total Time: 30 mins

Servings: 12

Ingredients

- 2 family size black tea bags
- 4 cups of boiling water
- 2 lemons, thinly split
- 1 cup of sugar
- 1 tbsp almond extract
- 2 tsp vanilla extract
- 1 (2 liter) bottle lemon-lime flavored carbonated beverage, chilled

Directions

3. Tea bags should be steeped in hot water for 15 Mins in a saucepan. Squeeze the lemon slices as you add them to a big pitcher as you wait for the tea to brew. Add the sugar.
4. Put the brewed tea, sugar, and lemons in a pitcher. This can be used immediately away or kept in the refrigerator for up to a day. Add lemon-lime soda, vanilla essence, and almond extract when ready to serve.

56.EMON MINT ICED TEA RECIPE

PREP TIME10 mins

FEFRIGERATE4 hrs

TOTAL TIME4 hrs 10 mins

INGREDIENTS

- 3 cups of good quality tea chilled
- 8 fresh mint leaves
- 1 lemon split
- 1 lime split
- Ice cubes

INSTRUCTIONS

1. Tea bags should be steeped in hot water for 15 Mins in a saucepan. Squeeze the lemon slices as you add them to a big pitcher as you wait for the tea to brew. Add the sugar.
2. Put the brewed tea, sugar, and lemons in a pitcher. This can be used immediately away or kept in the refrigerator for up to a day. Add lemon-lime soda, vanilla essence, and almond extract when ready to serve.

NUTRITION

1. Energy: 8 kcal 3g of carbohydrates 0.2g of protein Fat: 0.1g 0.01g of saturated fat 0.03g of polyunsaturated fat 0.1 g of monounsaturated fat Salt: 6 mg 94 milligrams of potassium 1g of fiber Sucrose: 0.3g 10 mg. calcium Iron: 0.2mg

57. LEMONADE-MINT ICED TEA

Prep Time: 25 mins

Total Time: 25 mins

Servings: 12

Ingredients

- 3 tbsp crushed fresh mint leaves
- 1 quart boiling water
- ½ cup of instant iced tea powder
- 1 cup of white sugar
- 2 quarts cold water
- 1 (6 ounce) can refrigerate lemonade concentrate, thawed

Directions

2. Mix the mint leaves, one quart of boiling water, instant tea powder, and sugar in a one-gallon pitcher. To dissolve sugar, stir. Tend to for fifteen Mins.
3. Add the cold water and lemonade concentrate while stirring. Serve with ice in large glasses. If desired, strain the mint leaves out.

58. LEM-TEA WHAMMY

Prep Time: 15 mins

Total Time: 15 mins

Servings: 8

Ingredients

- 4 cups of lemonade
- 4 cups of cold tea
- 2 tbsp white sugar

Directions

1. Stir tea and lemonade together in a big pitcher. Add sugar and mix until it dissolves. Refrigerator chill.

59. MATCHA FRAPPE

Prep Time: 5 mins

Total Time: 5 mins

Servings: 1

Ingredients

- 1 cup of milk
- 1 tsp matcha green tea powder, or more as need

- 5 ice cubes, or as needed
- 1 tbsp vanilla-flavored syrup (such as Torani®)
- 1 tbsp whipped cream, or as need

Directions

2. Blend the milk, ice, matcha green tea powder, and vanilla syrup in that order until the desired consistency is reveryed. Top with whipped cream before serving.
3. Kitchen Notes:
4. Depending on your preferences, you can add or remove ice to change the frappe's thickness. I prefer warm, icy beverages.
5. Please refrain from using the contents of green tea tea bags; matcha has a completely different flavor.
6. Almond milk, rice milk, or soy milk can be used in place of the milk. I've noticed that almond milk has a definite aftertaste.
7. This recipe's ingredient ratios are flexible; you can increase the amount of ice, matcha green tea powder, or vanilla syrup as needed to achieve the desired thickness or sweetness.

60.ICED MATCHA GREEN TEA LATTE

Prep Time: 1 minute

Total Time: 1 minute

Servings: 1 cup of

Ingredients

- 12 oz Milk of choice
- 2 tsp matcha powder
- 2 tsp Vanilla Syrup or honey, or sugar

- 1 cup of ice

Instructions

1. Add the milk, matcha powder, and vanilla syrup to the blender's container. Blend the matcha until it is completely lump-free, around 30 to 1 minute.
2. Pour over ice in a cup of, then enjoy!

Notes

1. *You can multiply or treble the recipe and keep the leftover matcha in the refrigerator for the remainder of the week.

61.ORANGE SPICE TEA MIX

INGREDIENTS

- 2cups of instant Tang orange drink (must be Tang, not Kool Aid)
- 1cup of instant tea, mix sweetened and lemon flavor
- 1 1/2cups of sugar
- 2tsp cinnamon
- 1tsp ground allspice
- 1tsp ground clov

DIRECTIONS

2. Mix all ingredients in a bowl. Use an airtight container for storage.
3. How to use: To a cup of or mug of boiling water, add approximately 2 heaping tbsp. Stirring vigorously

62.PERFECT PEVERY ICED TEA

PREP TIME10 Mins

COOKING TIME40 Mins

TOTAL TIME50 Mins

SIMPLE SYRUP

- 1 cup of organic cane sugar
- 1 cup of water
- 2 ripe peveryes (thinly split // + more for serving)
- TEA
- 2-3 Tbsp loose leaf black tea (3-4 tea bags // depending on how strong you prefer it)
- 8 cups of filtered water

Instructions

1. In a small saucepan, bring the sugar, water, and peveryes to a boil. After that, reduce the heat and whisk while crushing the peveryes to release their flavor.
2. Once the sugar has dissolved, cover the pan, turn the heat off, and let the mixture steep for 25–30 Mins.
3. Use a big pot or a tea maker to brew your tea in the interim. I use this IngenuiTEA loose leaf tea steeper. IMPORTANT: Try not to let it steep for more than 4-5 Mins as it will get bitter. Use less tea if you prefer it weaker or more tea if you prefer it stronger.
4. After brewing, take out the tea bags or drain the loose leaf tea into a pitcher. To chill, refrigerate.
5. Pour the resulting simple syrup into a bottle or other container over a fine mesh sieve to remove the peveryes. You can save the peveryes for later use, perhaps to top ice cream sundaes or oatmeal.

6. When ready to serve, either pour some simple syrup into the tea and stir, or pour all of the syrup into the tea and stir. I'd rather keep it apart. Tea should be served with fresh pevery slices over ice. The recipe makes approximately 10 servings as described (with ice and peveryes).

63.RANDY'S TEXAS TEA

Prep Time: 10 mins

Total Time: 10 mins

Ingredients

- 1 cup of white sugar
- ¼ tsp salt
- 1 cup of hot water
- 6 cups of brewed black tea, cold
- 2 cups of orange juice
- ½ cup of lemon juice
- 1 orange, split into rounds
- 1 lemon, split into rounds
- 1 lime, split into rounds

Directions

1. Mix sugar, salt, and hot water in a big pitcher. Stir until everything has dissolved. Lemon juice, orange juice, and tea, sir. Serve citrus fruit slices and ice in large glasses.

64.MONTANA TONIC

INGREDIENTS

- 4 cups of black tea, brewed
- 1 stick cinnamon
- 1/4 cup of white sugar
- 1 cup of raspberry juice
- 1 recipe - 1 lemon, juiced
- 1 sprig fresh mint
- 1 liter carbonated water

PREPARATION

2. Make cinnamon stick tea. In the boiling tea, dissolve the sugar. Set apart for cooling.
3. Mix the tea, raspberry juice, and lemon juice in a big pitcher. Add three crushed mint leaves and mix. Include the carbonated water.
4. Mix, then pour over ice.

65.COLD BREW PEVERY ICED TEA

prep time: 10 MINS

Cooking Time: 0 MINS

total time: 10 MINS

Ingredients

- 3 peveryes, split

- peel of 1 orange, peel off into large slices*
- 3 sprigs of mint
- 2–5 tsp organic cane sugar, maple syrup or honey
- 5 tea bags of earl grey tea
- 1-litre water

Instructions

1. The peveryes should be added to the bottom of a pitcher and lightly squashed with a wooden spoon.
2. Orange zest pieces, mint, your preferred sweetener, tea bags, and water should all be added. Mix everything.
3. For 6 to 12 hours, cover and place in the refrigerator.
4. Serve over ice after removing the tea bags.

Notes

1. Slice the orange peel with a vegetable peeler.
2. I usually add 3 tsp of maple syrup or cane sugar to the iced tea, but you can easily add more if you want yours sweeter.
3. I prefer to make this iced tea the night before and let it chill there. Strain the tea and remove (or eat, wonderful!) the peveryes if you like a clear iced tea.

66.SMOOTH SWEET TEA

Prep Time: 5 mins

Additional Time: 3 hrs 15 mins

Total Time: 3 hrs 20 mins

Ingredients

- 1 pinch baking soda
- 2 cups of boiling water
- 6 tea bags
- ¾ cup of white sugar
- 6 cups of cool water

Directions

1. Pour some baking soda into a 64-ounce heat-resistant glass pitcher. Tea bags are added after adding boiling water. For 15 Mins, cover the pot and let it steep.
2. Tea bags should be taken out and thrown away. Stir in sugar until it dissolves. Add cool water, and then chill for about three hours, or until cold.

3. Ingredients
4. Baking soda, 1 pinch
5. two glasses of hot water
6. six teabags
7. White sugar, 1/4 cup of
8. 6 cups of iced water
9. Local Deals Change 00000
10. Oops! There are no ingredients for sale nearby that we can find. Are we using the right zip code?
11. ADVERTISEMENT
12. Directions
13. Pour some baking soda into a 64-ounce heat-resistant glass pitcher. Tea bags are added after adding boiling water. For 15 Mins, cover the pot and let it steep.
14. Tea bags should be taken out and thrown away. Stir in sugar until it dissolves. Add cool water, and then chill for about three hours, or until cold.

67.APPLE SPICED TEA

Ingredients

- 1/2 cup of apple cider or juice
- 1/4 tsp chop up fresh gingerroot
- 2 whole allspice
- 2 whole cloves
- 1 black tea bag
- 1/2 cup of boiling water
- 1 tbsp brown sugar

Directions

1. Mix the first five ingredients in a small bowl. Add some hot water. For five Mins, cover and steep. Remove the tea bag and spices, then strain. Add sugar and mix. Serve right away.

68.APRICOT LEMONADE ICED TEA

Ingredients

- 4 cups of water
- 7 tea bags
- 1 cup of sugar
- 1 can (12 ounces) refrigerate lemonade concentrate, partially thawed
- 1 cup of chilled apricot nectar
- 4 cups of cold water
- Ice cubes
- Mint sprigs

Directions

2. Bring 4 cups of water to a boil in a saucepan; turn off the heat. tea bags; cover and steep for five Mins.
3. Throw away tea bags. Add sugar and stir until it is dissolved. Let it cool. Move to a pitcher and let cool completely.
4. Pour cold water into the tea after adding the nectar and lemonade concentrate. Serve with mint over ice.
5. Nutritional data
6. 148 calories, 0 fat (0 saturated fat), 0 cholesterol, 3 mg of sodium, 38 grams of carbohydrate (36 grams of carbohydrates, 0 fiber), and 0 grams of protein are in 3/4 cup of.

69.ARNIE'S GIMLET SLUSH

Ingredients

- Makes 4 Servings
- 6 ounces vodka
- 5 ounces simple syrup
- 4 ounces chilled brewed black tea
- 3ounces fresh lime juice
- Mint sprigs (for serving)

Preparation

1. Step 1 Blend the vodka, simple syrup, tea, and lime juice. Freeze for three to twelve hours (mixture will be partially refrigerate).
2. Step 2 Blend the ingredients with 2 cups of ice until it is thick and smooth. Divide among glasses, adding mint sprigs as a garnish.

70.BLACK CURRANT TEA WITH CINNAMON AND GINGER

INGREDIENTS

- 6cups of water
- 12wild black currant herbal tea bags
- 2(3 inch) long cinnamon sticks, broken in half
- 1tbsp packed chop up peel off fresh ginger
- 6tbsp refrigerate raspberry-cranberry refrigerate juice concentrate
- 1/4cup of sugar
- ice cube
- 8cinnamon sticks
- 8pieces crystallized ginger, rounds

DIRECTIONS

1. Using a big saucepan, bring 6 cups of water to a boil.
2. Tea bags, broken cinnamon sticks, and fresh ginger should all be added.
3. Get rid of the heat. For 10 Mins, cover and steep.
4. Add sugar and juice concentrate together. Cool off completely.
5. In a pitcher, strain the tea mixture. (May be made one day in advance. Cover and let stand.)
6. Add ice to 8 wineglasses. Add the tea mixture on top.
7. Ginger rounds and cinnamon sticks are used as garnish.

71.BERRY BERRY LEMONADE

Ingredients

- 7 tea bags
- 3 cups of boiling water
- 1/2 cup of fresh or refrigerate blueberries
- 1/2 cup of sugar
- 4 cups of cold water
- 3/4 cup of thawed raspberry lemonade concentrate
- 1 medium lemon, split
- Ice cubes

Directions

1. In a 4-cup of glass measuring cup of, put tea bags. As need, add boiling water and steep for 3 to 5 Mins. Throw away tea bags. a little tea cooling. Blueberries should be placed in a small food processor and blended until smooth.
2. Stirring the tea and sugar together will help the sugar dissolve. Add blueberries, lemon slices, lemonade concentrate, and cold water by stirring. Keep cold in the refrigerator. Serve chilled.

Ingredients

- 3 cups of fresh raspberries
- 1 cup of sugar
- 1 cup of packed fresh basil leaves, coarsely chop up
- 1/4 cup of lime juice
- 2 black tea bags
- 1 bottle (1 liter) carbonated water or 1 bottle (750 milliliters) sparkling rose wine
- Ice cubes
- Non-compulsory: Fresh raspberries and basil leaves

Directions

1. The raspberries, lime juice, sugar, basil, and large pot. Blend berries. Sauté the berries for 7 Mins over medium heat to release their juices.
2. Add tea bags after removing from the heat. 20 Mins of steeping under cover. Remove the raspberry seeds and tea bags before straining. Pour the tea into a 2-quart pitcher. Refrigerate until serving with a cover on.
3. Wine or carbonated water can be added gradually just before serving. Serve chilled. Add basil and raspberries as desired.

73.AUTUMN TEA

Ingredients

- 5 tea bags
- 5 cups of boiling water
- 5 cups of unsweetened apple juice
- 2 cups of cranberry juice
- 1/2 cup of sugar
- 1/3 cup of lemon juice
- 1/4 tsp pumpkin pie spice

Directions

1. Put the tea bags and boiling water in a sizable heat-resistant bowl. For 8 Mins, cover and steep. Throw away tea bags. Stir the tea with the remaining ingredients until the sugar is dissolved. either heated or above ice.

74.ARTILLERY PUNCH

Ingredients

- 1 cup of sugar
- Juice of 6 lemons
- 2 tbsp bitters
- 1 quart Sherry
- 1 quart Rye or Bourbon or Scotch
- 1 quart Brandy
- 1 quart Claret wine
- 1 quart Club Sode or 2 quarts sparkling Burgundy

Directions

1. In a punch bowl, mix all the ingredients and then add ice. Add another bottle of Coke or sparkling Burgundy to weaken the charge from 7 to 5 (charge 5).

75.APPLE CIDER VINEGAR TEA

Prep Time: 5 mins

Total Time: 5 mins

Ingredients

- 12 fluid ounces hot water, or more as desired
- 2 tbsp lemon juice
- 2 tbsp apple cider vinegar
- 1 tbsp raw honey
- 1 tsp ground cinnamon

Directions

2. In a sizable cup of, mix the hot water, honey, cinnamon, lemon juice, cider vinegar, and vinegar.

76.ALMOND LEMONADE TEA

INGREDIENTS

- 4cups of brewed tea
- 3cups of water
- 1(6 ounce) can refrigerate lemonade, thawed
- 1/4cup of sugar
- 1tsp almond extract

DIRECTIONS

3. Large pitcher with all the ingredients mixd; whisk until sugar melts. Rest of the tea should be chilled and served over ice.

77.AGUA FRESCA WITH WATERMELON AND POM TEA

Prep Time: 15 mins

Total Time:15 mins

Ingredients

- 1 seedless watermelon, rind removed and watermelon slice into chunks
- 2 tbsp lime juice
- 16 fluid ounces pevery-flavored iced tea (such as POM® Pomegranate Pevery Passion White Tea)
- 1 cup of water as needed

Directions

4. Lime juice is added to the blender after the watermelon has been well blended. Blend in the iced tea with a pevery flavoring. To get the appropriate strength, dilute with water.
5. Tips
6. Pour over ice and filter out the watermelon pulp for a thinner beverage. If desired, add extra water.
7. If you like, top up every glass with 1 ounce of rum (sugar cane is excellent, but any clear rum will do).

78.ADENI TEA

Prep Time: 10 mins

Cooking Time: 15 mins

Total Time: 25 mins

Ingredients

- 3 orange pekoe tea bags
- 3 cups of water
- ¼ cup of white sugar
- 10 cardamom seeds, or as need
- ½ tsp ground cinnamon
- ½ tsp ground nutmeg
- ½ tsp ground ginger
- 1 (12 fluid ounce) can evaporated milk

Directions

1. Tea bags should be slice open, emptied into a small dish, and then thrown away.

2. In a pot, bring water to a boil before adding loose tea. Simmer tea for 3 to 5 Mins, or until the water turns a dark crimson color. Tea with sugar added.
3. Use a mortar and pestle or an electric grinder to crush the cardamom seeds. Tea should be infused with ground cardamom, cinnamon, nutmeg, and ginger after being boiled for around 10 Mins.
4. Tea with milk added should be brought back to a boil for two Mins. Tea should be poured through a sieve to remove particles. Serve warm.

Cook's Notes:

1. By adding one cup of more or one less water, you can adjust the amount of milk in the mixture. If you want to make the most authentic version of this drink, feel free to add additional sugar since it is meant to be quite sweet. If you like, you can use freshly slice ginger root and cinnamon sticks, but I find the powders to have a stronger flavor. I use Lipton(R) yellow label tea bags for the tea.

79. THE BEST LEMON ICED TEA

Prep Time:5 mins

Additional Time:1 hrs

Total Time: 1 hrs 5 mins

Ingredients

- 4 green tea bags
- 4 orange pekoe tea bags
- 6 cups of boiling water
- 1 cup of white sugar
- 1 (12 ounce) can refrigerate lemonade concentrate
- ½ lemon, juiced
- 10 cups of cold water, or as needed

Directions

2. Put black and green tea bags in a 1-gallon glass pitcher or jar. Tea bags should be infused in boiling water for 30 Mins.
3. Take out the tea bags, then whisk in the sugar and lemonade concentrate until mixd. Add lemon juice and stir. Using cold water, completely fill the jar. Refrigerate until completely cold. Serve chilled.

80. THAI ICED TEA ชาเย็น (CHA YEN)

Ingredients

- 3 Tbsp (45 ml) Thai tea leaves (buy Thai tea leaves online)
- 1 cup of (240 ml) off-the-boil water
- 1.5 Tbsp (22 ml) sweetened condensed milk
- 2-3 tsp (10-15 ml) sugar
- A pinch of salt
- 1-2 Tbsp (15-30 ml) evaporated milk
- A lot of ice

Instructions

1. Thai tea leaves should be steeped in hot water for three to five Mins. You can either use a cloth filter bag, as in the video, or just steep the tea in a cup of before filtering it through paper.
2. Condensed milk, sugar, and salt should all be mixd in a mixing glass while the tea steeps. Pour the freshly brewed tea into the glass after stirring the sugar and condensed milk into the tea.
3. When ready to serve, add ice to a glass to the very top, then add the blended tea, leaving a little space on top.
4. Add some evaporated milk to the top and serve.

5. Note: If you wish to prepare the tea ahead of time and chill it before serving, think about adding a bit more water. Otherwise, the tea may be too thick or sweet and the ice may not melt as much when you pour cold tea over it. But remember as need and adjust as desired!

81. THAI ICED TEA (THAI TEA)

Prep Time5 mins

Cooking Time15 mins

INGREDIENTS

- ½ cup of Thai Tea Mix
- 2 ½ cups of water
- ¼ cup of granulated sugar
- Ice
- 1 cup of half and half - or milk of choice (full-fat coconut milk, sweetened condensed milk, evaporated milk, whole milk, etc.)

INSTRUCTIONS

1. In a little saucepot set over medium-high heat, bring water to a boil. Sugar and Pantai Thai Tea Mix should be added. To blend, stir. Boil gently for about two Mins on low heat before turning off the heat.
2. After letting the tea soak for 10-15 Mins, strain the liquid through a fine-mesh strainer to remove the particles. Leave the tea alone to cool (for best results, allow the tea to cool in the refrigerator for at least 1 hour).

3. Ice should be put in glasses. Thai tea should be poured into the cup of about two-thirds of the way, leaving space for milk or cream. Half and half (or the preferred milk of choice) should be poured into the glass and mixed together.
4. Excellent when consumed right away.

82.SWEET LIME ICED TEA

Prep Time: 10 mins

Cooking Time: 5 mins

Additional Time: 3 hrs 45 mins

Ingredients

- 1 gallon boiling water
- 6 black tea bags
- 1 ½ cups of white sugar
- 4 limes, juiced

Directions

1. Tea bags should be covered with boiling water in a gallon jar. 45 Mins should be given for steeping.
2. Take out and throw away the tea bags. Add sugar and lime juice, stirring until sugar dissolves. Refrigerate until chilled before serving after cooling to room temperature.

83.STARBUCKS MATCHA GREEN TEA FRAPPUCCINO

Ingredients

- 1/2 cup of whole milk
- 1 1/2 cups of small ice cubes
- 1 1/2 tbsp matcha powder (sweetened)
- 1 tbsp simple syrup
- 1 tbsp vanilla syrup
- 1/4 tsp xanthan gum
- 1/3 whipped cream (non-compulsory)

Instructions

1. In a 16 ounce cup of, add milk.
2. Ice cubes should almost completely fill the cup of.
3. On top of the ice, layer the remaining ingredients (except the whipped cream) and the sweetened matcha powder.
4. Once all the ice has been diced, add all the ingredients to a blender, and process for a full one to two Mins to give the xanthan gum time to emulsify the frappuccino.
5. In the same cup of used for measuring, pour the matcha green tea frappuccino and top with whipped cream.

84. SPRINGTIME CITRUS COOLER

Prep Time: 5 mins

Cooking Time: 5 mins

Total Time:10 mins

Ingredients

- 1 Earl Grey tea bag
- 1 medium orange, thinly split
- 3 tbsp white sugar
- 1 tsp rose water

Directions

1. The Earl Grey tea bag should steep for 5 Mins in a strong cup of tea. In a half-gallon pitcher, mix the tea, sugar, rose water, and orange slices. Pour cold water into the container and swirl to dissolve the sugar.

85. SPICED THAI ICED TEA

Prep Time: 5 mins

Cooking Time: 5 mins

Ingredients

- 5 cups of water

- ¼ cup of white sugar
- 5 pods star anise
- 1 cinnamon stick
- 4 pods cardamom, crushed
- 8 red rooibos tea bags
- ¾ cup of sweetened condensed milk
- ice

Directions

2. Bring to a boil the following ingredients: water, sugar, star anise, cinnamon stick, and cardamom. Add tea bags after removing from the heat. After about an hour, let the tea steep and cool to room temperature.
3. Remove tea bags, drain out whole spices, and throw them away. Condensed milk is whisked in. Pour into a sizable pitcher and chill for at least an hour to allow flavors to meld.
4. Add ice to 4 glasses. On ice, serve tea.

Cook's Note:

1. If you'd rather, you can swap the red rooibos with black tea with orange taste.
2. Use half a cup of loose tea instead of eight to ten tea bags when using loose tea. In the second step, strain through a cheesecloth or coffee filter positioned within a fine-mesh sieve.

86.SOUTH CAROLINA SWEET TEA

Prep Time: 1 mins

Cooking Time: 10 mins

Total Time: 11 mins

Ingredients

- 3 family size tea bags
- 2 cups of white sugar

Directions

1. With the aid of an electric coffee maker, The strainer basket should contain the 3 tea bags (not in the pot). Tea should be brewed similarly to coffee. Fill a pitcher with one gallon of sugar. Teakettle heated, pour in. Till you have enough tea to fill the pitcher, keep running the coffee machine while using the tea bags. Refrigerate after allowing to cool completely at room temperature.

87.SIMPLE BUBBLE TEA

Prep Time: 5 mins

Cooking Time:5 mins

Additional Time: 1 hrs

Total Time: 1 hrs 10 mins

Ingredients

- 4 cups of water
- 1 cup of quick cooking pearl tapioca
- 6 cups of brewed black tea
- ¼ cup of sweetened condensed milk
- 4 tsp white sugar, or as need
- ice cubes

Directions

2. Tapioca pearls should be added to boiling water before the kettle is covered. Medium-low heat should be used to simmer for 5 Mins. Drain the pearls and reserve them.
3. Condensed milk, sugar, and brewed tea should all be added to a pitcher and stirred to mix. Tea mixture should be cooled in the fridge for about an hour.
4. 4 big glasses should every have roughly 2 tsp of tapioca pearls. Add ice on top of the tea mixture in every glass.

88.ROSE HIP ICED TEA

Prep Time: 5 mins

Cooking Time: 5 mins

Total Time: 10 mins

Ingredients

- 4 cups of water
- 4 tbsp dried rosehips
- 1 tbsp sugar, or as need

Directions

1. Put water in a pot and bring to a boil. Rosehips should be added to boiling water, covered, and simmered slowly for five Mins.
2. With the heat off, add the sugar and whisk until it dissolves. For five Mins, keep covered while steeping.
3. Using a fine sieve, strain the tea. Transfer to a cool area before chilling in the refrigerator.

89.RASPBERRY ICED TEA

Ingredients

- 8-1/4 cups of water, separated
- 2/3 cup of sugar
- 5 tea bags
- 3 to 4 cups of fresh or refrigerate unsweetened raspberries

Directions

1. Bring 4 cups of water to a boil in a big pot. Add sugar and mix until it dissolves. Add tea bags after removing from the heat. For 5-8 Mins, steep. Throw away tea bags. Add 4 cups of water.
2. Bring the raspberries and remaining water to a boil in a separate pan. Lower heat; allow to simmer for 3 Mins, covered. Remove pulp, then discard it. juice from a raspberry to the tea mixture. Pour over ice in cold glasses.
3. Nutritional data
4. One cup of has 87 calories, 0 fat (0 saturated fat), 0 cholesterol, 0 sodium, 18g of carbohydrates, 3g of fiber, and 0g of protein.

90.RANDY'S TEXAS TEA

Prep Time: 10 mins

Total Time: 10 mins

Ingredients

- 1 cup of white sugar
- ¼ tsp salt
- 1 cup of hot water
- 6 cups of brewed black tea, cold
- 2 cups of orange juice
- ½ cup of lemon juice
- 1 orange, split into rounds
- 1 lemon, split into rounds
- 1 lime, split into rounds

Directions

1. Mix sugar, salt, and hot water in a big pitcher. Stir until everything has dissolved. Lemon juice, orange juice, and tea, sir. Serve citrus fruit slices and ice in large glasses.

91.PEVERY ORANGE ICED TEA

Prep Time: 10 mins

Additional Time: 1 hrs

Total Time: 1 hrs 10 mins

Ingredients

- 1 large fresh pevery, split
- 1 clementine, peel off and segmented
- 1 tbsp white sugar, or as need
- 8 cups of boiling water
- 4 Earl Grey tea bags

Directions

2. In a pitcher, mix sugar, pevery, and clementine. Using a spoon, mash the fruit; then, stir in the water and tea bags. For about one hour, refrigerate until cool. Using a slotted spoon, remove the fruit and tea bags.

92.MOJITEAS

Prep Time: 5 mins

Additional Time: 4 hrs 8 mins

Total Time: 4 hrs 13 mins

Ingredients

- 4 tea bags
- 12 sprigs fresh mint
- 3 cups of boiling water
- 1 cup of white sugar
- 1 cup of orange juice
- ¼ cup of lemon juice
- 3 cups of cold water, or more as need
- 1 cup of light rum, or more as need

Directions

3. In a large pitcher, add the tea bags and the mint sprigs. Add boiling water, then let it steep for 8 to 10 Mins. Remove the tea bags and mint, then squeeze any remaining tea back into the pitcher before discarding. Once the sugar has dissolved, add the orange and lemon juices and stir again. Add rum and cold water. Refrigerate for at least 4 hours and up to 24 hours.

93.MINT JULEP ICED TEA

Prep Time: 10 mins

Cooking Time: 5 mins

Additional Time: 10 mins

Total Time: 25 mins

Ingredients

- 1 cup of white sugar
- 1 cup of water
- 4 tea bags
- ½ cup of chop up fresh mint
- 2 quarts cold water
- 1 cup of orange juice
- 6 tbsp lemon juice

Directions

4. In a small saucepan, bring sugar and 1 cup of water to a boil while stirring constantly for 5 Mins or until sugar dissolves. To the sugar mixture, add the tea bags and the mint, and steep for 10 Mins. Remove tea bags and mint, then strain the mixture.
5. In a pitcher, mix the tea mixture, cold water, orange juice, and lemon juice.
6. Author's Note

7. When using the magazine version of this recipe, please be aware that some ingredient amounts have changed and that bourbon is used.

94. BLACK CURRANT TEA WITH CINNAMON AND GINGER

INGREDIENTS

- 6cups of water
- 12wild black currant herbal tea bags
- 2(3 inch) long cinnamon sticks, broken in half
- 1tbsp packed chop up peel off fresh ginger
- 6tbsp refrigerate raspberry-cranberry refrigerate juice concentrate
- 1/4cup of sugar
- ice cube
- 8cinnamon sticks
- 8pieces crystallized ginger, rounds

DIRECTIONS

1. Using a big saucepan, bring 6 cups of water to a boil.
2. Tea bags, broken cinnamon sticks, and fresh ginger should all be added.
3. Get rid of the heat. For 10 Mins, cover and steep.
4. Add sugar and juice concentrate together. Cool off completely.
5. In a pitcher, strain the tea mixture. (May be made one day in advance. Cover and let stand.)
6. Add ice to 8 wineglasses. Add the tea mixture on top.
7. Ginger rounds and cinnamon sticks are used as garnish.

95.CARAMEL-CHAI TEA LATTE

Ingredients

- 3-1/2 cups of water
- 1-1/2 cups of whole milk
- 10 chai-flavored black tea bags
- 1/3 cup of caramel flavoring syrup
- Sweetened whipped cream and hot caramel ice cream topping, non-compulsory

Directions

1. Water and milk should be brought to a boil in a big pot over medium heat while being stirred occasionally. Insert tea bags. Lower heat; simmer with lid on for five Mins. Remove from heat and steep for an additional five Mins covered.
2. Pour all of the tea's extra liquid into the cup of and then discard the tea bags. Add caramel syrup and stir. Serves may be garnished with whipped cream and caramel sauce, if preferred.

96.CARDAMOM CHAI

INGREDIENTS

- 2 tbsp.cardamom whole see note
- 2 tsploose tea black
- ¼ cup ofwater
- 1 cup ofwhole milk
- 1 tspsugar see note

INSTRUCTIONS

1. a milk pan with cardamom seeds added.
2. Insert loose tea.
3. add water
4. Bring the water to boil before letting it simmer until it is almost 2-3 tbsp.
5. the milk.
6. Put sugar in.
7. Use a fine strainer to pour the milk and tea, which have been cooking for about 5 Mins, into the serving cups of.
8. Enjoy it hot.

97.CHAI TEA CONCENTRATE

Prep Time: 5 mins

Cooking Time: 10 mins

Additional Time: 1 hrs

Total Time: 1 hrs 15 mins

Ingredients

- 4 cups of water
- 15 whole cloves
- 3 cinnamon sticks
- 8 (1/4 inch thick) slices unpeel off fresh ginger
- 15 cardamom pods, split
- 15 whole black peppercorns
- 10 black tea bags

- ⅓ cup of brown sugar
- 2 tsp vanilla extract

Directions

1. In a saucepan, bring water to a rolling boil. Add the cloves, and cook for one minute. Add tea, cardamom pods, peppercorns, ginger, cinnamon sticks, and ginger. After 6 Mins, pour the tea into a container. Stir in brown sugar and vanilla essence, then chill tea in the refrigerator for at least one hour.
2. Culinary Note:
3. To provide: approximately two parts concentrate to one part milk (almond milk works really well). Consume warm or with ice. For roughly a week, concentrate will remain safe in the refrigerator.

98.CHAMOMILE CREME ANGLAISE

Recipe Ingredients

- 2 1/2 cups of 592ml Half-and-half
- 8 Chamomile tea bags
- 8 Egg yolks (large)
- 1/3 cup of 65g / 2.3oz   Sugar

Recipe Instructions

1. Simmer half-and-half in a sturdy medium saucepan. Add tea bags and turn off the heat. 30 Mins of steeping under cover. Discard tea bags after straining mixture through strainer into bowl. Bring the half-and-half back to a simmer in the same pot.
2. In a medium bowl, mix egg yolks and sugar by whisking. Stir in the heated half-and-half gradually. Put mixture back in the same pan. Stir over low heat for about 15

Mins, or until sauce barely thickens (do not boil; sauce will be thin but will thicken slightly when cold). the next day, cover and chill. (May be made two days in advance. Remain chilled.) Offer chilled.

3. About 2 cups of this recipe's output.

99.CHAMOMILE PANNA COTTA WITH QUINCE

PREP:0 HR

COOK:0 HR

TOTAL:0 HR

INGREDIENTS

- Small quinces (about 3 pounds)
- 1 bag chamomile tea
- 4 wide strips lemon zest
- 1 cup of sugar
- 1/2 vanilla bean, split lengthwise
- 1 tbsp fresh lemon juice
- 1 cup of plain whole-milk Greek yogurt
- 1 1/2 cups of heavy cream
- 1 1/2 cups of whole milk
- 2/3 cup of sugar
- Pinch of kosher salt
- 4 bags chamomile tea
- 2 tsp unflavored powdered gelatin
- Eight 6-ounce glasses or ramekins

INSTRUCTIONS

1. Step 1: To remove fuzz off quinces, rub them with a damp paper towel. No need to peel, core, or remove seeds from the remaining 2 quinces; simply slice the remaining 4 into large pieces. Put the quince pieces in a big saucepan and cover with cold water. Until quinces are extremely soft, simmer for 60 to 75 Mins, adding more water as required to keep covered. Bring to a boil. Reduce heat. Discard particles after straining cooking liquid into a big bowl. Clean the pot, then set it aside.
2. Step 2: Peel the reserved quinces and separate the flesh from the cores into four lobes (be careful; core is very hard). Add tea bag, lemon zest, sugar, and quince boiling liquid to the saucepan you set aside. Add pod after scraping in vanilla seeds. Cook for 45–60 Mins, stirring regularly, until quinces are a deep pinkish-red and soft and the liquid is syrupy after bringing to a boil. Let quinces cool in the syrup, then add lemon juice and mix. eject the pod.
3. Do it now
4. Step 3 Quinces can be stolen five days in advance. Cover and let stand.
5. assembling and panna cotta:
6. Step 4 Whisk heavy cream into the yogurt in a medium basin while adding the heavy cream gradually.
7. Step 5 Stirring constantly, bring milk, sugar, and salt to a simmer in a small saucepan over low heat. Add the vanilla seeds and the pod after adding the tea bags. Remove from heat and allow it stand for 15-20 Mins to allow flavors to meld.
8. Step 6: In the meantime, dissolve the gelatin in 1/4 cup of cold water and leave it to sit for 10 Mins to soften.
9. Step 7
10. Just before steaming, reheat the milk mixture over medium-low. After removing from the heat, whisk in the gelatin to dissolve it. Remove particles and strain into a bowl with the yogurt mixture. until smooth, whisk. Distribute evenly among glasses or ramekins after pouring. Set panna cotta in the refrigerator for at least 4 hours. Serve with syrup and quinces that have been poached.
11. in advance
12. Step 8
13. Make the panna cotta two days in advance. Keep refrigerated and covered.

100.CHINESE SPARERIBS

Prep Time: 5 mins

Cooking Time: 40 mins

Additional Time: 2 hrs

Total Time: 2 hrs 45 mins

Servings: 2

Ingredients

- 3 tbsp hoisin sauce
- 1 tbsp ketchup
- 1 tbsp honey
- 1 tbsp soy sauce
- 1 tbsp sake
- 1 tsp rice vinegar
- 1 tsp lemon juice
- 1 tsp grated fresh ginger
- ½ tsp grated fresh garlic
- ¼ tsp Chinese five-spice powder
- 1 pound pork spareribs

Directions

1. In a shallow glass dish, mix the hoisin sauce, ketchup, honey, soy sauce, sake, rice vinegar, lemon juice, ginger, garlic, and five-spice powder. Turn the ribs in the dish to coat them. For two hours or up to overnight, cover and marinade the food in the refrigerator.
2. Set the oven to 325 degrees Fahrenheit (165 degrees C). Water should be added to a broiler tray so that it covers the bottom. Ribs should be arranged on the grate, which should be placed over the tray.

3. Cook for 40 Mins on the center rack of a preheated oven while flipping and bashing with marinade every ten Mins. 10 more Mins of cooking the marinade will create a glaze. If preferred, finish under the broiler. Throw away any leftover marinade.

101.CHOCOLATE CHAI FRAPPES

Ingredients

- 4 chai tea bags
- 1/2 cup of boiling water
- 2 cups of 2% chocolate milk
- 1/2 cup of ice cubes
- 4 dashes ground cinnamon
- 4 dashes ground nutmeg

Directions

1. Boiling water should be added to the tea bags in a small bowl. 15 Mins or until lukewarm, let stand.
2. Throw away tea bags. Tea should be added to a blender along with milk and ice. For 30 seconds, or until slushy, cover and process. Pour into glasses of cold water. Add a few dashes of nutmeg and cinnamon before serving right away.

102.DARK CHOCOLATE EARL GREY TRUFFLES

Prep Time: 0 min

Cooking Time: 20 min

Total Time: 20 min

INGREDIENTS

- 1 cup of whipping cream
  10 ounces Caraïbe Couverture
  2 ⅛ tbsp honey
  1.6 ounces (1 tbsp) butter
  ½ ounce Earl Grey tea
  2 tsp orange flower water*
  Valrhona Cocoa Powder

INSTRUCTIONS

1. Bring the honey and tea-infused cream to a boil.
2. Pour one-third of the hot liquid on top of the chocolate when it has melted to 105°F (41°C). Stir until the mixture is elastic and glossy, add 1/3 of the cream, mix quickly to re-emulsify, and then add the final 1/3 of the cream.
3. Using a hand mixer, mix the softened butter and orange flower water until the ganache is glossy and smooth.
4. Spoon the mixture into a sheet pan with borders, then cover with plastic wrap.
5. Wait until the ganache is cold enough to slice into cubes (several hours in the refrigerator or overnight at room temperature).
6. Serving of sifted Valrhona Cocoa Powder is used to roll them in.
7. Best in Class

8. Base of Form

103.CINNAMON APPLE REFRESHER

Ingredients

- 4 cups of boiling water
- 5 cinnamon-apple herbal tea bags
- 1-1/3 cups of cranberry juice
- 2 tbsp sugar
- Apple slices, non-compulsory

Directions

1. Pour boiling water over tea bags in a teapot; cover and steep for five Mins. Grab the luggage. Add sugar and cranberry juice after that. Add liquid to glasses. If desired, add apple slices as a garnish.

104.CRANBERRY TEA

Ingredients

- 2 ½ quarts water
- 1 (32-ounce) jar cranberry juice cocktail
- ¼ cup of lemon juice
- 2 cups of sugar
- 4 (3-inch) cinnamon sticks
- 1 tbsp whole cloves
- 3 family-size tea bags
- 1 cup of orange juice

- Garnish: fresh mint sprigs

Directions

2. In a big Dutch oven, bring the first 6 ingredients to a boil. Next, turn down the heat, and simmer for 10 Mins. Add tea bags, turn off the heat, cover, and let steep for five Mins. Tea bags, cinnamon, and cloves should be taken out and thrown away before adding orange juice with a slotted spoon. With lemon slices, serve over ice after chilling. If desired, add a garnish.

105.CITRUS ICED TEA

Prep:15 mins

Ingredients

- 6 ordinary tea bags
- 2 tbsp caster sugar
- 10 sprigs mint
- 300ml fresh orange juice
- juice 1 lime
- 1/2 split orange, mint leaves and ice to serve

Method

3. STEP 1 Prepare the tea with the sugar and 1.2 liters of water. Infuse the kettle with mint for 10 Mins. Drain, then cool.

4. STEP 2 Pour the mixture into a jug, add the juices, and whisk to mix. Garnish with orange slices, mint, and lots of ice.

106.CITRUS ICED TEA WITH MINT

Ingredients

- 8 cups of water, separated
- 6 tea bags
- 1 to 2 mint sprigs
- 3-1/2 tsp Crystal Light lemonade drink mix
- 2 cups of orange juice
- Ice cubes

Directions

1. 1 qt. of water should be brought to a boil in a Dutch oven. Add mint and tea bags. For ten Mins, cover and steep. Remove the tea bags and mint, then strain.
2. Mix the remaining water and the lemonade mix in a big container. Add the tea and orange juice and stir. Cool. Serve chilled.

INGREDIENTS

- 10 Sunkist oranges
- 1 1/2 cups of sugar
- 1 tbsp whole cloves
- 5 cinnamon sticks
- 3 tbsp loose black tea
- 2 Sunkist lemons, split
- 1 can pineapple juice

DIRECTIONS

1. Peel five oranges, then reserve the zest.
2. Juice all 10 oranges, then reserve juice.
3. Save aside half of the freshly squeezed orange juice for later use.

4. Put the cooked zest aside after briefly sautéing it over medium heat until aromatic.
5. Five oranges' worth of juice should be added to a pot along with a sprinkle of sugar. Cook over medium heat until reduced by about half. Zest is then added to the juice.
6. Orange juice and zest should be removed from the heat and placed aside.
7. Bring to a boil 8 cups of water, 8 cinnamon sticks, and the cloves. Remove from heat after 10 Mins of boiling.
8. Steep black tea for 10 Mins after adding. Using a strainer, separate the cinnamon sticks, cloves, and

108.CITRUS PUNCH

Prep: 5 min. + chilling

Ingredients

- 2 cups of pineapple juice
- 2 cups of orange juice
- 1 cup of grapefruit juice
- 1 cup of lemonade
- 2 cups of ginger ale, chilled

Directions

1. Juices and lemonade should be mixd in a sizable pitcher. Keep cold in the refrigerator. Pour into a punch bowl just before serving. Add ginger beer gradually.

109.CITRUS TEA WITH TARRAGON

Ingredients

- For Citrus Tea With Tarragon
- 1/2 c
- orange juice
- 1/4 c
- honey
- 1/4 c cold water
- 3 Tbsp lemon juice
- 2 Tbsp lime juice
- 1/2 c packed fresh tarragon leaves
- 8 cups of water
- 4

- 4 earl grey tea bags
- orange slices (non-compulsory)
- fresh tarragon sprigs (non-compulsory)

110.MAKE

2. Orange juice, sugar, honey, 1/4 cup of cold water, lemon juice, and lime juice should all be mixd in a small pot. Over a medium-high heat, bring to a boil while stirring continuously. Take the pan off the heat and let it stand for 15 Mins.

3. Blenderize the citrus combination. Add 1/2 cup of tarragon leaves; mix for 30 seconds with the lid on. Use cheesecloth that is twice as thick to line a strainer with a fine mesh. Citrus mixture should be sieved, and any solids should be discarded.

4. Bring the 8 cups of water to a boil in a big pot. Get rid of the heat. Add tea bags and brew for five Mins. Take out and throw away the tea bags. Mix the tea with the strained citrus mixture. Orange slices and tarragon sprigs should be used to garnish every serving.

111.COLD BREW PLUM ICED TEA

Ingredients

- 8 black tea bags
- 3 large sprigs lemon verbena or mint, + more for serving
- 1 cup of sugar
- 4 large red plums, slice into thin wedges
- 2 tbsp fresh lemon juice

Step

1. In a big pitcher, mix tea bags, 3 lemon verbena sprigs, and 8 glasses cold water. For at least 8 and up to 12 hours, cover and chill.
2. In the meantime, heat 1 cup of water and sugar to a boil in a medium pot. Simmer for 10 Mins after adding plums and reducing heat. After 30 Mins, remove from heat and let soak. Pour the lemon juice into a small basin after straining the plum syrup. For at least 30 Mins, cover and refrigerate until cold.
3. Tea bags and lemon verbena sprigs should be removed from the tea before adding 3/4 cup of plum syrup and 4 cups of ice. Pour in glasses with ice and more lemon verbena as a garnish.
4. Do it now
5. Making the syrup for plums takes a day. Remain cold.

112. CRANBERRY HERBAL TEA COOLER RECIPE

Ingredients:

- 3-1/2 cups of water
- 1/2 cup of orange juice
- 2 tbsp sugar
- 8 orange spice herbal tea bags
- 4 cups of reduced-calorie reduced-sugar cranberry juice
- orange slices

Directions:

1. Bring the water, orange juice, and sugar to a boil in a small saucepan. For 10 Mins, simmer with the heat reduced and the lid on. Add tea bags after removing from the heat. Allow to stand for four Mins.
2. Take out and throw away the tea bags. Add cranberry juice after transferring to a pitcher. Keep cold in the refrigerator. Orange slices are a nice garnish. 8 servings in the yield.

113.HOT CRANBERRY TEA

Cooking Time: 1 hrs 30 mins

Total Time: 1 hrs 30 mins

Servings: 14

Ingredients

- 3 ½ quarts water
- 1 (12 ounce) package cranberries
- 2 cups of white sugar
- 2 oranges, juiced
- 2 lemons, juiced
- 12 whole cloves
- 2 cinnamon sticks

Directions

1. Water and cranberries should be mixd in a big pot. Stirring often, bring to a boil, then simmer for 30 Mins. Add sugar, lemon, orange, and clove juices as well as cinnamon sticks. For one hour, cover and steep.

114.CRANBERRY-MINT TEA RECIPE

Ingredients

- 8 cups of water
- 1 bag (12 ounces) fresh or refrigerate cranberries
- 6 black tea bags
- 1½ cups of fresh mint leaves, + extra sprigs for garnish
- Organic sugar as need (non-compulsory)

Directions

2. Bring water, cranberries, and tea bags to a boil in a big pot. Reduce heat to low, cover, and simmer for 10 Mins once cranberries start to pop, which should take around 5 Mins. Five more Mins of simmering topped with mint. Pour tea into a heatproof pitcher using a fine-mesh sieve, pressing cranberries to extract as much juice as you can; discard solids. If preferred, stir in 14 cup of sugar at a time, tasting as you go. Serve hot in mugs with fresh mint sprigs for decoration. If you'd prefer to serve it cold, whisk in an additional 2 cups of water, chill in the refrigerator until chilled, then serve over ice with fresh mint sprigs as a garnish.

115.CUCUMBER TEA SPRITZER

Prep Time: 10 mins

Cooking Time: 5 mins

Additional Time: 5 mins

Total Time: 20 mins

Servings: 5

Ingredients

- 2 cups of water
- ½ cup of white sugar
- 2 black tea bags, or more as need
- ice
- 1 cucumber, slice into 1/4-inch slices
- 5 cups of sparkling water, or as needed
- 1 lemon

Directions

3. In a kettle, bring water to a boil. Add liquid to a pitcher. Add sugar and stir till it turns into syrup. Add the tea bags and steep them for 5 Mins.
4. Ice cubes should be put in 5 glasses. Add some pieces of cucumber. Glasses should be 3/4 full of sparkling water. Give every glass of sweet tea the same amount. Add some lemon juice and whisk into every beverage.

116.CURRIED CHICKEN SALAD SANDWICHES

Prep/Total Time: 20 min

Ingredients

- 2 cups of cubed cooked chicken breast
- 3/4 cup of chop up apple
- 3/4 cup of dried cranberries
- 3/4 cup of mayonnaise
- 1/2 cup of chop up walnuts
- 1/2 cup of chop up celery
- 2 tsp lemon juice
- 1 tbsp chop up green onion

- 1 tsp curry powder
- 6 lettuce leaves
- 6 croissants, split

Directions

1. Chicken, apple, cranberries, mayonnaise, walnuts, celery, lemon juice, onion, and curry powder should all be mixd in a big bowl. assemble croissants with lettuce. Add the chicken salad mixture on top.
2. Nutritional data
3. 625 calories, 41g fat (10g saturated fat), 84mg cholesterol, 614mg sodium, 43g carbohydrate (14g sugars, 4g fiber), and 21g protein are contained in 1 sandwich.

117.DAIRY HOLLOW HOUSE'S FAMOUS HERBAL TEA COOLER

INGREDIENTS

- FOR COOLER
- Water (use bottled spring water if your tap water doesn't taste good)
- 1 box (20 bags) of Red Zinger, Raspberry Zinger, or other hibiscus- and rose hip-based herbal tea (read ingredient list on the box)
- 1 (12-ounce) container refrigerate apple juice concentrate, no sugar added, thawed and undiluted
- 1 cup of freshly squeezed orange juice (from about 4 oranges)
- FOR GARNISH
- Ice
- Split rounds of orange
- Split half-rounds of lemon and lime
- Sprigs of fresh mint

DIRECTIONS

1. 4 cups of (1 quart) of water should come to a hard boil. Drop in all 20 tea bags after turning the heat off. until the liquid reveryes room temperature, steep (tea can even steep overnight).
2. The tea bags should be fished out and squeezed with clean hands to extract every last flavorful drop.
3. Add one additional cup of cold water, along with the thawed, undiluted apple juice concentrate and fresh orange juice.
4. Put in a glass pitcher.
5. When it's time to serve, place glasses on the table and top every with a slice of orange, lemon, or lime and a sprig of mint. Ice is then added to the glasses. Pour cooler over ice and give it a moment to stand (cooler is quite concentrated, but the ice dilutes it just right).

118.DELUXE SPICED TEA MIX

Prep/Total Time: 10 min

Ingredients

- 2 jars (20 ounces every) orange breakfast drink mix
- 1-3/4 cups of sugar
- 1 envelope (.23 ounce) unsweetened lemonade Kool-Aid mix
- 1 jar (3 ounces) unsweetened instant tea
- 2-1/4 cups of Red Hots
- 2 tsp every ground allspice, cinnamon, cloves and nutmeg

Directions

1. Mix all ingredients in a jar with a tight seal. Storage for up to six months in a cool, dry location. Produce: 10 cups of (about 120 servings).

2. Tea preparation: Pour 1 cup of boiling water over 4 tsp of the mixture and whisk thoroughly.
3. Nutritional data
4. four tsp 16g carbohydrate (15g sugars, 0 fiber), 0 protein, 66 calories, 0 fat (0 saturated fat), 0 cholesterol, 17mg sodium.

119.DON'S SIMPLE SWEET TEA

Prep Time: 5 mins

Cooking Time: 10 mins

Additional Time: 1 hrs

Total Time:1 hrs 15 mins

Servings: 10

Ingredients

- 8 cups of water
- 4 family-sized tea bags
- 2 cups of white sugar

Directions

1. In a pot, bring water to a boil. Boiling water with sugar dissolves; turn off the heat.
2. Tea bags should be brewed for 3 to 5 Mins, depending on the desired strength of tea.
3. Tea should be chilled for at least one hour.

120.DREAMSICLE ICED TEA LATTE

Prep Time: 10 mins

Cooking Time: 10 mins

Additional Time: 5 mins

Total Time: 25 mins

Servings: 2

Ingredients

- 4 cups of water, separated
- 1 cup of brown sugar
- 2 tbsp almond extract
- 1 tsp vanilla extract
- 3 cups of almond milk
- 4 orange herbal tea bags

Directions

1. Brown sugar and 1 cup of water should be mixd in a pot. Bring to a boil while stirring continuously. Add vanilla and almond extracts after removing from the heat.
2. Bring the remaining water and almond milk to a boil in a saucepan. Add tea bags and brew for five Mins. Take out the tea bags and then add the extract mixture. Pour tea into two large cups of after adding ice.

121.DUCK BREASTS WITH ORANGE, HONEY AND TEA SAUCE

Ingredients

- Makes 4 servings
- 2 boneless Muscovy duck breast halves (about 1 3/4 pounds total)
- 3/4 cup of chop up shallots
- 2 1/4 cups of canned low-salt chicken broth
- 1 1/2 cups of orange juice
- 4 1/2 tsp Earl Grey tea leaves or 5 tea bags, leaves removed from bags
- 1 tbsp honey
- 3 tbsp butter, slice into small pieces
- Orange segments (non-compulsory)

Step

1. set the oven to 450 degrees. Using a fork, prick the skin of the duck breasts all over. Put some salt and pepper on the duck. Large, hefty skillet on high heat. Place the skin-side down duck breasts in the skillet. Sauté for about 4 Mins, or until skin is nicely browned. Cook duck breasts for two Mins on the other side. Get rid of the heat. Put a rack inside a roasting pan. Put the duck breasts on the rack (reserve drippings in skillet). For medium-rare, roast the duck for around 20 Mins.

2. Over medium heat, reheat the drippings in the skillet. Add the shallots and cook for about 5 Mins, or until they start to brown. Letting the drippings flow to the lower end, tilt the skillet and push the shallots to the higher end. Drips should be removed and discarded. To the skillet, add the broth, orange juice, and tea leaves. Boil for 17 Mins or until mixture is reduced to 1 1/4 cups of. Strain the mixture through the strainer over the bowl while pressing down on the particles to get as much liquid out as you can. Waste the sediments in the strainer. liquid back into the same skillet. Add honey and boil for a while. Butter is whisked in. Use salt and pepper to season the sauce.

3. Crosswise, thinly slice the duck breasts. Place equal amounts of slices on every of the four dishes. Around the duck, spoon sauce. If desired, garnish with orange segments.

122.EARL GREY RUM PUNCH

Total Time:15 mins

Hands-on Time:5 mins

Hands-on Time:5 mins

Ingredients

- 4 cups of water
- 3 tbsp Frontier Co-op Fair Trade Organic Earl Grey Black Tea
- 8 Frontier Co-op Cinnamon Sticks
- 1/4 cup of light brown sugar
- 2 cups of apple cider
- 1 1/2 cups of spiced dark rum
- 8 cinnamon sticks and orange slices, for garnish

Directions

1. Bring water to a boil in a kettle, then steep tea for four to five Mins (or to your preferred strength).

2. Pour tea through a strainer or into a punch bowl.

3. 8 cinnamon sticks, the brown sugar, apple cider, and rum should all be added. Leave out the garnishes.

4. Pour over ice into eight highball glasses to serve cool. Add an orange slice and a cinnamon stick as garnish.

5. Pour into eight heated Irish coffee glasses or mugs to serve warm. For a richer hot toddy, stir in a little melted butter and top with an orange slice and cinnamon stick.

123.EARL GREY TEA ICE CREAM

Ingredients

- Makes about 1 quart
- 2 cups of heavy cream
- 1 cup of whole milk
- 3/4 cup of (150 grams) sugar
- 6 tbsp (30 grams) loose Earl Grey tea
- 1/2 tsp (2 grams) kosher salt
- 6 large egg yolks

Step

1. Place a double boiler or a heatproof bowl over a pot of gently simmering water. Pour the cream and milk into the boiler or bowl (the bottom of the bowl should not touch the water). Tea, salt, and 1/2 cup of (100 grams) of the sugar should be whisked in. Continue stirring until the salt and sugar are completely dissolved. The mixture should be heated until steam is rising from the top. Take the mixture from the heat and squeeze the tea leaves to extract as much of the infused liquid as you can before straining it into a bowl. Return the infused dairy mixture to the double boiler after discarding the tea leaves.
2. In the meantime, make an ice bath in a big bowl and place another bowl on top of it. Set aside.
3. In a medium bowl, mix the egg yolks and the remaining 1/4 cup of (50 grams) of sugar and whisk until smooth. Place a kitchen towel below to prevent slippage. Add a small amount of the hot dairy mixture to the yolks while stirring. Up until you've added about half of the dairy mixture, keep adding it while mixing it in. In the double boiler, mix the remaining dairy mixture with the yolk mixture. When steam starts to rise from the surface and the custard has thickened enough to coat the back of the spoon, turn the heat beneath the double boiler to medium and cook the custard, stirring frequently with a wooden spoon and turning down the heat as needed. While holding the spoon horizontally, sift the custard with your finger. The custard is prepared for cooling if the fingerprint trail you leave behind doesn't reappear.

4. After making the ice bath, strain the custard into the bowl over it and stir for 3 to 5 Mins, or until the custard has cooled. The custard should be transferred to a quart-sized container, covered, and chilled for at least 4 hours or ideally overnight.

5. Use an ice cream maker to freeze the chilled custard in accordance with the manufacturer's instructions. So that you may use it to store the completed ice cream, put the container you used to refrigerate the custard in the freezer. The ice cream should be blended until it resembles "soft serve." Once in the cooled storage container, transfer the ice cream there and let it freeze until it reveryes the appropriate consistency. You can also serve it right away; it will have the consistency of gelato. When refrigerate, the ice cream can last up to 7 days.

124.ELDERBERRY BLOSSOM TEA

Ingredients

- 1 to 2 tbsp dried elderberry blossoms or 2 to 3 tbsp fresh elderberry blossoms
- 1 cup of boiling water
- Sugar as need
- 1 thin lemon slice

Directions

1. Elderberry blooms should be steeped in boiling water for 5–10 Mins in a tea cup of or mug before straining. Add lemon and sugar.

125.ESPECIADO COCKTAIL

Ingredients

- Makes 16 cocktails
- 2 cups of dried hibiscus flowers
- 1 cup of (packed) light brown sugar
- 4 sprigs rosemary
- 8 cloves whole cloves
- 6 allspice berries
- 2 cinnamon sticks, + more for serving
- 3 star anise pods, + more for serving
- 12 ounces tequila or mezcal
- 8 lemon slices, halved

Preparation

2. Step 1 Put 12 cups of water, hibiscus, brown sugar, rosemary, cloves, allspice berries, 2 cinnamon sticks, and 3 star anise pods to a boil. Cook for 50–60 Mins, or until reduced by half. Discard sediments after straining through a fine-mesh sieve into a large bowl. Hibiscus combination should be chilled for at least four hours.
3. Step 2 Mix cooled hibiscus concoction with tequila, then pour into rocks glasses with ice. Add a lemon slice, a star anise pod, and a cinnamon stick to the top of every cocktail.
4. Making the hibiscus combination up to 4 days in advance is step 3. Keep refrigerated and covered.

126.ETHIOPIAN SPICE TEA

Ingredients

- Serves 1
- 1 tsp ground cardamom
- 1/2 tsp ground cinnamon
- 1/8 tsp ground nutmeg
- 1/8 tsp ground cloves
- 1 cup of water
- 1 (1/4-inch-thick) slice fresh ginger

Step

1. In a small dish, mix all of the ground spices together.
2. Water is brought to a boil. Add ginger and 1/8 tsp of the spice mixture, then boil for 4 Mins. Pour tea into a cup of and strain it through a fine sieve lined with a coffee filter or paper towel.

127.FISH HOUSE PUNCH

Ingredients

- Makes about 10 cups of
- 1 cup of sugar
- 3 1/2 cups of water
- 1 1/2 cups of fresh lemon juice (6 to 8 lemons), strained
- 1 (750-ml) bottle Jamaican amber rum
- 12 oz Cognac (1 1/2 cups of)
- 2 oz pevery brandy (1/4 cup of)
- Garnish: lemon slices

Special Equipment

1. a cardboard juice or milk carton with the top (spout) end removed.
2. Step 1 Fill a carton with water and freeze it until it becomes solid, which should take around 8 hours (see the cooks' comment, below).
3. Step 2 In a large dish or pot, stir together the sugar and 3 1/2 cups of water until the sugar is completely dissolved. Add brandy, Cognac, rum, and lemon juice; cover and chill for at least three hours.
4. Step 2 In a large dish or pot, stir together the sugar and 3 1/2 cups of water until the sugar is completely dissolved. Add brandy, Cognac, rum, and lemon juice; cover and chill for at least three hours.
5. Step 3: Place an ice block in a punch bowl and top with punch.

128.FLAMING HOLIDAY PUNCH RECIPE

Active:15 mins

Total:45 mins

Serves:20 servings

Ingredients

- Save Recipe
- 6 small oranges
- Approximately 1/2 cup of whole cloves
- 1/2 tsp ground cinnamon
- 1/2 tsp ground allspice
- 1/2 tsp ground nutmeg
- 1/4 cup of sugar, as need
- One 750ml bottle aged rum
- 1/2 gallon apple cider
- 1 pint boiling water (non-compulsory, should you wish for further dilution)

Directions

1. the oven to 350 degrees. By forcing the clove's pointed end through the orange peel until just the bud protrudes, you can stud an orange with whole cloves. Continue with the remaining oranges and bake for 30 Mins or until tender. Put the oranges in a heat-resistant punch bowl once they have somewhat cooled.
2. Place the bottle of rum in a pot of hot (but not boiling) water for around ten Mins to warm it up. Heat the cider in a sizable saucepan until steaming, then pour it into a pitcher and set it aside while the rum warms.
3. Add sugar to the punch bowl after adding the rum. Turn off the lights.
4. Scoop up a little of the rum using a heatproof ladle. Light the scoop of rum with a kitchen match while holding the ladle away from the punch bowl (and your face, the drapes, and the dog); if necessary, add a little high-proof rum to aid in ignition.

5. Drizzle the flaming rum into the punch bowl with caution; this should light the remaining rum. Spices should be added in little amounts to the flames.
6. Douse the flames after a few Mins, or whenever you've had enough of the display, by slowly pouring hot cider (and hot water, if using), stirring as you go. The flames might not go out right away, but if you keep stirring, they will eventually flicker and go out as the alcohol is diluted.
7. Use punch cups of to serve.

129.REFRIGERATE BOOZY ARNOLD PALMER

Ingredients

- Makes 4
- 8 black tea bags, preferably English breakfast
- 5 tbsp sugar
- 3 1/2 cups of store-bought or homemade lemonade, separated
- 1 cup of vodka, separated
- Lemon wheels (for garnish)
- Special Equipment
- 4 ice cube trays

Step

1. In a medium saucepan, heat 3 1/2 cups of water until it is boiling. Remove from heat and stir in sugar and tea bags. Steep for 4 Mins. Tea should make about 3 1/2 cups of; discard tea bags and allow tea to cool slightly.
2. In two ice cube trays, divide 3 cups of tea; chill the remaining 1/2 cup of. Chill the final 1/2 cup of lemonade and divide 3 cups of among the remaining 2 ice cube trays. Refrigerate for 3–4 hours or until solid.
3. In a blender, mix 1/2 cup of vodka, 1/2 cup of lemonade, and blend until completely smooth. Add to a pitcher or spouted liquid measuring cup of. The remaining 1/2 cup of tea, 1/2 cup of vodka, and the blender jar have been rinsed. Blend the ingredients until smooth.
4. Half-fill a big glass with the lemonade mixture and tilt the glass to one side. Pour in refrigerate tea mixture to fill glass and create a swirl as you slowly raise the glass to the upright position. Lemon wheels are a tasty garnish.

5. Do it now
6. Make ice cubes three months in advance. Place in freezer-safe plastic bags and seal.

130.REFRIGERATE CHAI LATTE

Ingredients

- 1 1/2 cup of chai tea
- 2 tbsp vanilla syrup
- 1/2 cup of milk
- 1 cup of ice
- caramel and whipped cream for topping

Instructions

1. Blend everything together (except the caramel and whipped cream).
2. Once smooth, blend.
3. Enjoy after adding caramel and whipped cream to the top!

131.EASY HOMEMADE ICED TEA

Prep Time: 20 Mins

Cooking Time: 0 Mins

Total Time: 20 Mins

Servings: 8

Ingredients

- 8 tea bags
- 1.5 liters (6 cups of) boiling water
- 1 liter (4 cups of) juice of your choice
- 2 cups of fresh fruit and herbs of your choice

Instructions

1. The tea bags should be covered with boiling water and given 5 Mins to brew. Take out the tea bags, then let them cool. Add some ice to the brewed tea to quicken the chilling process.
2. After it has cooled, add the fruit juice on top of the cooled tea in a big jug. Serve with your choice of fruit and ice.

Nutrition

1. 57 kcal of energy, 14g of carbohydrates, 5 mg of sodium, 126 mg of potassium, 12g of sugar, 10 mg of calcium, and 0.1 mg of iron.

132.GIN TEA AND LEMON FIZZ

Ready In: 15mins

Ingredients: 6

INGREDIENTS

- 1cup of water
- 4tsp black tea bags (such as Darjeeling)
- 1cup of refrigerate lemonade concentrate, thawed
- 1cup of gin

- 2cups of sparkling water
- ice cube

DIRECTIONS

2. Put 1 cup of water to boil in a small saucepan. Add tea bags.
3. Get rid of the heat. Cover and let soak for 15 Mins.
4. Cold overnight.
5. Pour tea into a pitcher; discard tea bags.
6. Add lemonade concentrate and gin, then sparkling water to pitcher; whisk to mix.
7. Serve over ice.

133.GINGER ALE ALMOND TEA

Prep/Total Time: 5 min.

Ingredients

- 2 cups of diet ginger ale, chilled
- 2 cups of cold water
- 1/4 cup of sugar-free instant lemon iced tea mix
- 1/2 tsp almond extract
- 1/2 tsp vanilla extract

Directions

1. Mix all ingredients in a pitcher. Serve right away with ice.

134.GINGER CARDAMOM TEA

Prep/Total Time: 25 min.

Ingredients

- 2 cups of water
- 4 tsp honey
- 1 tbsp chop up fresh gingerroot
- 1/2 tsp ground cardamom
- 6 tea bags
- 1-1/2 cups of fat-free milk

Directions

2. Bring water, honey, ginger, and cardamom to a boil in a small saucepan. Simmer for ten Mins on low heat.
3. Pour into a 2-cup of glass measuring cup of and top with tea bags. 3 to 5 Mins, depending on preference. Throw out the ginger and tea bags before re-entering the tea into the pot. Add milk and heat thoroughly.

135.GINGER LEMON ICED TEA

Prep Time: 5 Mins

Cooking Time: 10 Mins

Total Time: 15 Mins

Servings: 2 servings

Ingredients

- 3 Black tea bags I used Lipton
- 1/4 cup of lemon juice
- 1/4 cup of honey
- 1 inch piece of ginger
- 1 cup of water.
- 18 to 20 pieces ice cubes
- Lemon slices

Instructions

1. Heat water in a pot or kettle.
2. Add tea bags and ginger to a large mug. Pour hot water into the cup of.
3. After submerging the tea bags many times, let it steep for ten Mins.
4. Include honey and lemon juice after removing the tea bags. Mix thoroughly.
5. Ice cubes, a few lemon slices, and 2 glasses should be filled. Over the ice cubes, pour the hot tea. Stir thoroughly, then sip.

Notes

6. The ice tea mix can be prepared in advance and stored in the refrigerator. It can keep for up to a week in the refrigerator.

136.FRESH GINGER TEA

Prep Time: 1 minute

Cooking Time: 9 Mins

Total Time: 10 Mins

INGREDIENTS

- 1-inch chunk of fresh ginger (no need to peel), split into pieces no wider than ¼-inch
- 1 cup of water
- Non-compulsory flavorings (choose just one): 1 cinnamon stick, 1-inch piece of fresh turmeric (slice into thin slices, same as the ginger), or several sprigs of fresh mint
- Non-compulsory add-ins: 1 thin round of fresh lemon or orange, and/or 1 tsp honey or maple syrup, as need

INSTRUCTIONS

1. Water and ginger slices are mixd in a pan over high heat. Add a cinnamon stick, fresh turmeric, or fresh mint at this time if you're including them. After bringing the

mixture to a simmer, turn down the heat if needed to keep it there for five Mins (for extra-strong ginger flavor, simmer for up to 10 Mins).

2. Take the pot off the stove. Pour the mixture either into a mug or a heat-safe liquid measuring cup of after carefully passing it through a mesh sieve.

3. Serve with a squeeze of lemon and/or a drizzle of honey or maple syrup, as desired. Serve warm.

NOTES

1. TURN IT VEGAN Use maple syrup and not honey, please.
2. Prepare beforehand: To create a large quantity, multiply the recipe as needed. For up to 4 days, cover and refrigerate leftovers after they have cooled to room temperature. Tea may be served hot or cold.
3. ROTTEN GINGER? Ginger can be refrigerate for later use. Before freezing the ginger, you might as well slice it thinly if you plan to use it later in tea. For additional adaptability, freeze it whole instead.

137.GINGER TEA RECIPE

Total Time: 22 Mins

INGREDIENTS

- 3 cups of hot water
- one 2-inch knob of fresh ginger root
- fresh lemon juice from 1/2 of a lemon
- ¼ tsp turmeric
- 1 tbsp raw honey or pure maple syrup (non-compulsory)
- pinch of cayenne pepper or a cinnamon stick (non-compulsory)

INSTRUCTIONS

1. Slice up a 2-inch knob of fresh ginger root extremely thinly after washing it. Peeling is non-compulsory, but you should scrape any obvious dirt off.
2. Depending on how powerful you want it to be, add the ginger slices to hot water and boil for 10 to 20 Mins.
3. Take the tea off the heat and strain it through a fine strainer to remove all of the ginger. Throw away the bits of ginger and, to improve flavor and health benefits, add your choice of cayenne, lemon, turmeric, raw honey, or maple syrup. Slice the turmeric root thinly if using, then boil it with the ginger.
4. Your fresh ginger tea is available in both hot and cold variations. Any sur+ should be kept in the fridge for one to two days. To get the most health advantages, consume one to three cups of daily.

138.GOLDEN GLOW PUNCH

Prep10 Min

Total0 Min

Ingredients

- 1(6-oz.) can refrigerate lemonade concentrate, thawed
- 1(6-oz.) can refrigerate orange juice concentrate, thawed
- 1(6-oz.) can refrigerate tangerine juice concentrate, thawed
- 2cups of cold water
- 2(33-oz.) bottles ginger ale, chilled
- Ice cubes or ice mold

Steps

1. Juice concentrates and water should be well mixd in a sizable nonmetal pitcher or punch bowl.
2. 2 Add ginger ale and ice right before pouring; mix to mix. Decorate as desired.

139. GREEN CHAI SPA TEA BLEND

Ingredients

- Makes 1 cup of tea blend
- 1/4 cup of Chinese green tea leaves
- 1/4 cup of whole green cardamom pods
- 1/4 cup of whole cloves
- 3 or 4 three-inch cinnamon sticks, coarsely chop up with a heavy-duty knife
- (Essential oil complement: orange)

Step

1. Place the tea, cardamom, cloves, and cinnamon sticks in a quart-sized plastic bag. As though inflating a balloon, blow into the bag. After inflated, tighten the bag and shake the herbs together. Keep in a container made of opaque ceramic or glass that has a tight-fitting lid or cork. Before removing any components, give the jar a vigorous shake to evenly disperse the contents. Use within six months for the best aroma.

Mixture of herbal tea with aromas:

2. Use 1/3 cup of dried lavender flowers, 1/3 cup of dried peppermint leaves, 1/3 cup of dried rose petals, and 1/3 cup of dried peppermint leaves as directed in the recipe for Green Chai Spa Tea Mix. (Rose essential oil is a compliment.)
3. Mixture of Stimulating Herbal Tea:
4. Use 1/3 cup of every of 1/3 cup of dried rosemary leaves, 1/3 cup of dried lemon balm leaves, and 1/3 cup of dried eucalyptus leaves in the Green Chai recipe. (Eucalyptus is a complementary essential oil.)

140. GREEN GODDESS KIWI COCKTAIL

PREP TIME: 5 MINS

Ingredients

- 1/2 kiwi, peel off
- 2 ounces premium gin
- 3/4 ounces St. Germain elderflower liqueur
- 1/2 ounce freshly squeezed lime juice
- 1 ounce simple syrup (see Notes)
- Soda water
- Kiwi slice (unpeel off), for garnish

Instructions

1. Component addition To break down the kiwi, muddle it in a cocktail shaker. Add gin, lime juice, simple syrup, elderflower liqueur, and.
2. Shake. Shake the shaker until it becomes frosty after adding ice and covering it. Pour cocktail into a Collins glass filled with ice (or tall cocktail glass).
3. Serve. Add soda water on top, then add a kiwi slice as a garnish.

Notes

1. Stir together equal amounts sugar and water to create simple syrup. Slowly warm the mixture while stirring over low heat until all the sugar has melted. Before using, cool.
2. If you want more pulp in your drink, you can omit the straining step.
3. Peli Peli provided the recipe.

141.IRISH WHISKEY GREEN TEA PUNCH

Prep Time: 5 Mins

Total Time: 5 Mins

INGREDIENTS

- 8 cups of brewed green tea, 8 cups of water, 5 tea bags
- 1/2 cup of fresh lemon juice
- 1 cup of ginger ale
- 1/2 cup of honey, more if you like it sweeter!
- 1½ cups of Jameson Irish Whiskey
- Mint leaves for garnish

INSTRUCTIONS

1. Put a heat-resistant bowl with the boiling water in it.
2. Ten Mins of steeping are required after adding 5 green tea bags.
3. After removing the tea bags, mix all the ingredients. Whisk to thoroughly mix everything and give the honey time to melt.
4. Large square ice cubes should be added if serving it cold about five Mins prior to your guests' arrival. Also, adjust this recipe to your tastes!
5. When needed, increase the whiskey, lemon, and honey.

142. GREEN TEA CHEESECAKE

Ingredients

- Makes 8 servings
- Cake
- 1 cup of (generous) ground shortbread cookies (about 6 ounces)

- 2 8-ounce packages cream cheese, room temperature (do not use whipped or "light" products)
- 1/2 cup of (packed) fromage blanc*
- 3/4 cup of + 2 tbsp sugar
- 4 large eggs
- 2 tsp Japanese green tea powder** or 2 tsp lightly ground green tea from about 4 tea bags
- Tisane
- 2 1/2-pint containers fresh red raspberries
- 2 1/2-pint containers fresh golden raspberries
- 1 bunch fresh mint
- Boiling water
- For cake:

Step

1. Set the oven to 325 F. Firmly press cookie crumbs onto the bottom of an 8-inch springform pan (not the sides). 3 layers of thick foil should be tightly wrapped around the pan's exterior. Cream cheese, fromage blanc, and sugar should be thoroughly blended in a large basin using an electric mixer. One at a time, add the eggs, beating well after every addition. Add the green tea powder and blend well. On the prepared crust in the pan, pour batter. Put the cake in the roasting pan and fill the roasting pan with hot water until the edges of the springform pan are halfway up.
2. Cake should be baked for about an hour, or until the middle is set but the pan shakes softly. Take the cake out of the pan and let it cool for an hour at room temperature. Overnight refrigeration is recommended. (May be made two days in advance. Keep chilled and covered.)
3. Using tisane:
4. Eight heatproof glasses should every include three mint leaves and five mixed red and golden raspberries. Boiling water should be used to fill the cups of.
5. To release the cake from the pan, slice around the sides. Put the cake on the dish. Add some raspberries as a cake garnish. wedges from the cake. Every slice should be served with a glass of tisane and a few raspberries.
6. Several supermarkets, cheese shops, and specialized food businesses sell fromage blanc.
7. **Japanese markets carry green tea powder.
8. Test-kitchen advice

143.STARBUCKS GREEN TEA FRAPPUCCINO

Prep Time10 mins

Total Time10 mins

Ingredients

- 10 ice cubes
- 1 cup of (8oz/240 ml) full fat milk
- 1 tsp vanilla extract
- 3 tbsp powdered sugar
- 1 ½ tbsp premium Japanese matcha-green tea powder

Instructions

1. All components should be blended in a blender until they are evenly smooth, creamy, and colored.
2. Enjoy right away.

144.GREEN TEA (MATCHA) ICE CREAM RECIPE

Prep:30 mins

Cook:8 hrs

Total:8 hrs 30 mins

Servings:4 to 6 servings

Ingredients

- 1 tbsp matcha green tea powder
- 3 tbsp hot water
- 2 large egg yolks
- 5 tbsp granulated white sugar
- 3/4 cup of whole milk
- 3/4 cup of heavy cream, whipped

Steps to Make It

assemble the components.

1. Matcha tea powder and boiling water should be mixd in a small bowl before setting it aside.

2. In a medium-sized saucepan, add the egg yolks and stir them just until mixd. Don't start heating the pan just yet.
3. Put sugar in the pan and mix it thoroughly with the egg yolks.
4. Mix thoroughly as you gradually add milk to the egg and sugar mixture.
5. Heat the egg mixture in the pan over low heat while continually swirling to prevent burning.

6. As the mixture begins to somewhat thicken, turn off the heat and immerse the pan's bottom in ice water to help the egg mixture cool.
7. Mix well before adding the matcha powder and water combination to the egg mixture. The mixture should continue to chill in ice water.
8. Beat the heavy cream until it reveryes the desired thickness and airiness.
9. Add this heavy cream that has been beaten to the egg and matcha mixture. Use a spatula to slowly mix all the ingredients together.
10. Follow the ice cream maker's churning instructions after adding the ice cream ingredients to the machine.
11. After that, transfer the mixture to a lidded freezer-safe container and freeze for at least eight hours before serving.

145.GREEN TEA MARGARITA

Ingredients

- 1/2 lime or lemon, slice into wedges
- Sea Salt (Grinder), enough to trim glass rim
- lemon zest, enough to trim glass rim
- ice cubes
- 1 oz tequila
- 1 oz limoncello liqueur
- 1/2 cup of Hibiscus Bliss Herbal Tea Blend, or green tea of your choice, prepared, chilled
- 4 tbsp lime or lemon juice

Preparation

1. A wedge of lime or lemon should be used to wet the rim of the margarita glass. On a small plate, sprinkling sea salt and lemon zest. Invert the glass in the trimmer while gently turning to evenly "frost" the rim. Set aside.
2. The other components should be mixd in a cocktail shaker. If you're using a highball glass, add extra tea.
3. After a thorough shake, pour into the prepared glass. Add a wedge of lime or lemon as garnish.

146.HEMP MILK CHAI

Ingredients

- 4 servings
- HEMP MILK
- ½ cup of hemp seeds
- SUPERDUST (NON-COMPULSORY)
- 2 tsp chlorella powder
- 1 tsp reishi or cordyceps powder
- ¼ tsp ground cardamom
- CHAI AND ASSEMBLY
- 2 3-inch cinnamon sticks
- 1 ½-inch piece ginger, peel off, lightly grated
- 16 cardamom pods
- Very small pinch of kosher salt
- 4 bags strong black tea
- 3 tbsp pure maple syrup

Preparation

1. Blend 3 cups of cold water and hemp seeds in a blender until very smooth. Pour into an airtight container after passing through a fine-mesh sieve (a cheesecloth sheet or nut-milk bag also work).
2. Hemp milk can be prepared five days in advance. Cover and let stand.
3. SUPERDUST
4. In a small bowl, mix the chlorella, reishi, and cardamom.
5. Assembly and Chai

6. In a sizable pot over medium-high heat, bring 2 cups of water, salt, ginger, cardamom pods, and cinnamon sticks to a boil. Simmer for 10-15 Mins with a cover on, on low heat, until extremely fragrant. Take heat off and stir in tea. for five Mins while covered.
7. In a clean saucepan, pass the chai mixture through a fine-mesh sieve. Add 2 cups of the hemp milk and the maple syrup; reserve the remaining hemp milk for later use. Cook over medium heat, stirring occasionally until just heated. Share among cups of, then sprinkle with superglue.

147.HIBISCUS ICED TEA

Ingredients

- 6 cups of water
- 1 cup of dried hibiscus flowers
- 1/3 cup of superfine sugar

Directions

1. Using a medium saucepan, bring water to a boil. Include hibiscus blooms. Turn off the heat and let the dish stand for an hour. Through a sieve; remove blossoms; strain. Add sugar and mix. Refrigerate for a minimum of one hour.

148.HIBISCUS-LEMON AGUA FRESCA

ngredients

- Makes about 7 cups of
- 1 cup of dried hibiscus flowers or 10 hibiscus tea bags
- 1/4 cup of sugar or agave syrup
- 2 tbsp fresh lemon juice

Step

2. In a big pot over high heat, bring hibiscus, sugar, and 8 cups of water to a boil. Ten Mins of simmering on low heat. If using hibiscus flowers, pour mixture into a large bowl using a fine-mesh sieve; discard particles. If using tea bags, remove bags and dump mixture into a big dish. Cool for at least two hours before serving. Pour slowly into a pitcher so that any little particles stay in the bowl before transferring. Add lemon juice and stir.
3. Do it now
4. For up to five days, aqua fresca can be chilled in an airtight container.

149.HIBISCUS-MARINATED LEG OF LAMB RECIPE

Ingredients:

- 1 quart water

- 3 large garlic cloves, peel off and smashed
- 10 black peppercorns, coarsely cracked
- 1 cup of dried nontoxic and organic hibiscus flowers (1 1/2 oz) or 20 bags red zinger tea leaves (1 box), removed from bags
- 1/4 cup of sugar
- 1 6- to 8-lb leg of lamb , with aitch bone (rump bone) removed by butcher
- 2 tbsp olive oil
- 1 tbsp red currant jelly
- 2 tbsp cold unsalted butter , slice into piece

Directions:

1. Making a marinade Using peppercorns and garlic, bring water to a boil. After adding, gently simmer for 5 Mins. After 30 Mins, turn off the heat and let the marinade steep. Pressing on the sediments as you pour the marinade through a fine sieve into a bowl, discard the solids. Stirring until sugar is dissolved, add the sugar and then refrigerate until chilled.
2. Lamb can be marinated by trimming off the majority of the fat and placing it in two layers of sealable plastic bags with the marinade. Lamb should be marinated for 12 to 24 hours in a refrigerated bag, rotating it occasionally.
3. Roast lamb: Take the lamb out of the bag, saving the marinade, and place it in a roasting pan that is just big enough to accommodate it. After oiling and patting the lamb dry, liberally sprinkle it with salt and pepper.
4. set the oven to 450 degrees. Place the lamb in the top third of the oven and lower the heat to 350°F. Roast for 1 to 1 1/2 hours, or until a thermometer reads 125°F when placed into the thickest portion of the leg (but not touching the bone).
5. The lamb should be transferred to a platter, covered with foil, and let to stand for 15 to 25 Mins (internal temperature will increase to around 135°F).
6. Pour the reserved marinade into the roasting pan as the lamb is still standing. Boil marinade while scraping out brown pieces in a skillet that is straddled over two burners until it has reduced to about 1 cup of.
7. Add any excess meat juices to the dish, mix in the jelly, and season with salt and pepper as need. Shake or stir the pan when adding the butter to incorporate it. To serve with lamb, pour sauce into a sauceboat after passing through a fine sieve.

150.HIBISCUS-MINT GRANITA

Ingredients

- Serves 4
- 6 dried hibiscus flowers, about 1/2 ounce
- 3/4 cup of sugar
- Juice of 1 lime
- 1/4 cup of chop up fresh mint leaves
- 4 whole fresh mint leaves

Method:

1. Step 1: Start by boiling 2 cups of water. After 5 to 7 Mins, remove from the heat and steep the hibiscus blossoms in the liquid. Toss the hibiscus blooms away. Stir the sugar into the boiling water until it dissolves. To dissolve the sugar, you might need to put it back on the fire for a minute or two. Turn off the heat and allow the food to cool to room temperature. Lime juice and chop up mint leaves should be added.
2. Step 2 Place a small bowl with the liquid in the freezer. Mash the big chunks of ice about every 30 Mins while the food is refrigerate for three to four hours.
3. Building: Step 3
4. Place the granita in chilled glasses and top with entire mint leaves as a garnish.

151.HOLIDAY WASSAIL PUNCH

Prep: 10 min. Cook: 4 hours

Ingredients

- 4 cups of apple juice
- 4 cups of orange juice
- 2 cups of cranberry juice
- 1 can (11.3 ounces) pineapple nectar
- 1/2 cup of sugar
- 2 tsp lemon juice
- 3 to 4 cinnamon sticks (3 inches)
- 8 whole allspice
- 8 to 10 orange slices
- Non-compulsory: Apple slices and fresh cranberries

Directions

1. Mix the first 6 ingredients in a 5- or 6-qt slow cooker. Put the allspice and cinnamon sticks on a double layer of cheesecloth. To surround the seasonings, gather the cloth's corners and tie a knot in the string. Orange slices and a spice package should be put in a slow cooker. For 4-5 hours, cook covered on low to let the flavors meld.
2. Throw away the orange segments and spice bag. Punch can non-compulsoryly be garnished with apple and cranberry slices. Serve hot.

152. HONEY-CITRUS ICED TEA

Prep: 15 min. + chilling

Ingredients

- 4 tea bags
- 2 cups of boiling water
- 3 medium navel oranges
- 2 medium lemons
- 2 cups of orange juice
- 1/4 cup of lemon juice
- 3 tbsp honey
- 1 liter ginger ale, chilled
- Ice cubes

Directions

1. In a teapot, add boiling water after adding the tea bags. Tea bags should be thrown away after 3 Mins under cover. Fill a pitcher with tea. Add two oranges, separated, and one lemon to the tea. Add honey, orange juice, and lemon juice after stirring. Overnight or for six hours, cover and chill. Slice the remaining orange and lemon; freeze.
2. Tea should be strained and the fruit discarded right before serving. Add ginger ale and stir. Serve with ice and refrigerate fruit slices.

153.HONEY LEMON GINGER TEA

Prep Time: 5 mins

Cooking Time: 10 mins

Total Time: 15 mins

INGREDIENTS

- 1 cup of honey
- 3 pieces lemons
- 3 tbsp fresh ginger
- Shop Recipe

INSTRUCTIONS

1. 3-lemon pieces
2. To remove wax, place the lemons in a strainer and cover with boiling water. After that, move to a basin of ice or room temperature water, rinse, and scrub the exterior skin. Dry the lemons with a fresh kitchen towel.
3. 3-lemon pieces
4. Lemons should be quartered lengthwise. Take the seeds out. Now, slice the lemon as thinly as you can (including the skin). Set aside.
5. 30 grams fresh ginger
6. By scraping the skin off the ginger with the edge of a spoon, the skin can be removed. Towel dry after rinsing. The ginger can be grated using a coarse grater (grater with slightly larger holes) or slice into very small cubes.
7. Three lemons, three tbsp raw ginger, and one cup of honey

8. Half the honey should be added to the jar along with the ginger and lemon, and the mixture should be stirred. Remix after adding the remaining lemon, ginger, and honey.

9. To let the flavors to meld, seal the jar and place it in the refrigerator for at least one night.

10. Give the jar a good shake or mix before using it as the honey can settle at the bottom. A cup of should include a tsp of the mixture and boiling water.

154.HONEY-PEAR ICED TEA

Prep: 15 min. + chilling

Ingredients

- 6 green chai tea bags
- 3 cups of boiling water
- 3 cups of pear nectar
- 1/3 cup of lemon juice
- 1/3 cup of honey
- Thin pear slices

Directions

1. Tea bags should be discarded after 3 Mins of tea infusion. Cool. Keep cold in the refrigerator.
2. Pear nectar, lemon juice, honey, and cooled tea should all be mixd in a pitcher. Add a slice of pear on the top of every serving.

155.HOT RUM & GINGER TEA TODDY RECIPE

Prep Time: 10 Mins

Cooking Time: 15 Mins

Total Time: 25 Mins

Servings: 2 Beverages

Ingredients

- 2 ½ cups of brewed orange pekoe tea
- 3 ounces dark rum
- 2 tsp agave nectar or honey
- 2 slices orange
- 2 thick peel off slices fresh ginger
- ¼ tsp ground nutmeg

Instructions

1. Mix the tea, rum, agave nectar (or honey), orange, ginger, and nutmeg in a small saucepan over medium heat.
2. Stir the mixture for 15 Mins while heating it up over medium heat. After being taken off the heat, the mixture should rest for about five Mins.
3. Take out the orange and ginger pieces, pour the mixture into two cups of, and top every with an orange slice to serve.

156.HOT SPICED GREEN TEA

Prep/Total Time: 15 min.

Ingredients

- 2 cinnamon sticks (3 inches)
- 4 green tea bags
- 1/2 tsp chop up fresh gingerroot
- 1/2 tsp grated lemon zest
- 4 cardamom pods, crushed
- 4 cups of boiling water
- 2 tbsp honey

Directions

1. Mix the first five ingredients in a big bowl. Add some hot water. For 5–6 Mins, cover and steep. Discard tea bags and spices after straining. Tea with honey in it. Serve right away.

157.HOT SPICED TEA

Prep/Total Time: 15 min.

Ingredients

- 2 cinnamon sticks
- 6 to 12 whole allspice
- 1 tsp whole cloves
- 12 cups of water
- 12 tea bags
- 1 cup of packed brown sugar
- 1 cup of cranberry juice
- 1/2 cup of orange juice
- 1/4 cup of lemon juice

Directions

2. On a double layer of cheesecloth, arrange the cinnamon sticks, allspice, and cloves. Tie a string to construct a bag by raising the corners of the fabric.
3. Bring to a boil the water and spice bag in a big pot. Take it off the heat. tea bags; cover and let steep for five Mins. Discard the spice and tea bags. Brown sugar should be dissolved by stirring. Add the juices and fully heat. Provide hot.

158.HOT TEA PUNCH

6 Servings

10m Prep Time

20m Cooking Time

30m Ready In

Ingredients

- Add to Shopping List
- 6 cups of water
- 1/4 cup of granulated sugar
- 2 cinnamon sticks
- 8 whole cloves
- 5 tea bags
- 1 1/2 cups of orange juice
- 1/3 cup of lemon juice

Step

1. Bring the first four ingredients (water, cloves, and a big pot of water) to a boil while stirring constantly until the sugar dissolves. 5 to 10 Mins of boiling. Get rid of the heat.
2. Tea bags are added, covered, and steeped for 10 Mins. Throw away tea bags.

3. Add the juices (orange and lemon).
4. Can be prepared a day in advance; cover and chill. Before continue, reheat; this can be done in a crockpot.
5. Remove entire spices with a slotted spoon.
6. Serve warm.

159.ICED CRANBERRY-MINT TEA

Prep: 20 min. + standing

Ingredients

- 4 cups of water
- 2/3 cup of loosely packed fresh mint leaves
- 2 tbsp sugar
- 8 lemon herbal tea bags
- 3-1/2 cups of reduced-calorie reduced-sugar cranberry juice
- 1 tbsp lemon juice
- Ice cubes
- Lemon slices, non-compulsory

Directions

1. Bring the water, mint, and sugar to a boil in a big saucepan. Add tea bags after removing from the heat. 15 Mins of steeping under cover.
2. Throw away tea bags. for a further 45 Mins while covered. Discard the mint leaves after straining. Lemon and cranberry juice are added to the tea. If preferred, serve with lemon slices over ice.

160.ICED HONEYDEW MINT TEA

Prep/Total Time: 20 min.

Ingredients

- 4 cups of water
- 24 fresh mint leaves
- 8 green tea bags
- 2/3 cup of sugar
- 5 cups of diced honeydew melon
- 3 cups of ice cubes
- Additional ice cubes

Directions

1. Bring water to a boil in a big pot, then turn off the heat. Tea bags and mint leaves should be added. Cover the mixture and let it soak for 3 to 5 Mins, stirring every so often. Eliminate the tea and mint bags. Add sugar and mix.
2. In a blender, mix 2-1/2 cups of honeydew, 2 cups of tea, and 1-1/2 cups of ice. Cover and mix until smooth. Serve on top of more ice. Add the remaining ingredients and repeat.

161.ICED LEMON AND GINGER DRINK

Ingredients

- 2 whole lemons, split
- 1 handful ginger, peel off and split
- 3 heaped tbsp brown sugar
- 2L boiling water
- 2 sprigs of mint, to serve

Method

1. Put sugar, ginger, and lemons in a sizable heat-resistant jug. Pour the boiling water on top.
2. When the flavors meld, let the mixture cool to room temperature. If necessary, taste and add more sugar; then chill until chilled.
3. In order to serve, fill every glass with ice and a few mint leaves.

162.GINGER & LEMON ICED TEA

Ingredients

- 75g ginger
- 2 tbsp Co-op clear honey

- 1 lemon
- 2 Co-op 99 blend Fairtrade tea bag
- Ice cubes
- Rosemary or thyme sprig, to serve

Method

1. Ginger should be peel off and coarsely chop up before being added to a big jug with honey and lemon juice.
2. Depending on how strong you prefer your tea, add the tea bags to 1 liter of boiling water and stir for 30 to 1 Mins.
3. Take out the tea bags and let them fully cool.
4. Remove the ginger from the cooled liquid before straining.
5. To serve, pour into tall glasses, top with ice cubes, and top with every a rosemary or thyme sprig and a slice of ginger.

163.ICED MELON MOROCCAN MINT TEA

Prep/Total Time: 20 min.

Ingredients

- 2 cups of water
- 12 fresh mint leaves
- 4 green tea bags
- 1/3 cup of sugar
- 2-1/2 cups of diced honeydew melon
- 1-1/2 cups of ice cubes
- Additional ice cubes

Directions

1. Bring water to a boil in a big pot. Add mint and tea bags after removing from the heat. For 3 to 5 Mins, cover and steep. Eliminate the tea and mint bags. Add the sugar and stir.
2. Blend the honeydew in a blender until smooth. Process the tea and 1-1/2 cups of ice until well mixd. Serve on top of more ice.

164.ORANGE ICE TEA

Total: 30 min

Prep: 5 min

Inactive: 20 min

Cook: 5 min

Ingredients

- Syrup:
- 1 cup of orange juice
- 1/2 cup of sugar
- Tea:
- 2 cups of water
- 7 black tea bags (recommended: Red Rose)
- 3 cups of sparkling water, chilled
- 1/2 small orange, thinly split
- Ice
- Fresh mint or basil sprigs, to garnish

Directions

1. specialized tools: a pitcher that holds 60 ounces (7 1/2 cups of)

2. The syrup needs: Orange juice and sugar should be heated to a boil in a small saucepan over high heat. For about 5 Mins, simmer, stirring now and again, until the sugar has dissolved. Turn off the heat and let the food cool for 20 Mins.
3. To make the tea: Bring the water to a boil in a little pan. After adding the tea bags, turn off the heat under the pan. Let the tea 20 Mins to steep and cool to room temperature. Take out and throw away the tea bags. When ready to serve, pour the tea and syrup into a pitcher and place in the refrigerator.
4. Orange slices should be added to the pitcher along with the sparkling water for serving. In 4 cups of with ice, pour the tea. Serve with fresh basil or mint garnish.

165.ICED MATCHA LATTE RECIPE

Prep Time: 5 mins

Total Time: 5 mins

INGREDIENTS

- 2 tsp matcha powder
- 1 to 2 tbsp hot water
- 1 cup of warm water
- Ice
- Milk of choice (I used almond milk)

INSTRUCTIONS

1. Add the matcha powder to a cup of or bowl for measurement. Add the 1 to 2 tsp of boiling water and stir until the matcha is completely dissolved. This should produce something that resembles a paste.
2. Mix, then add the final cup of water. Place in the freezer or refrigerator to chill for approximately 15 Mins.
3. Add your preferred milk to two glasses that have been filled with ice to about 3/4 of the way. This is an excellent opportunity, if you'd like, to add any simple syrup. Next, add the iced matcha and mix.

166.STRAWBERRY ICED TEA RECIPE

Prep Time: 10 Mins

Total Time: 10 Mins

Ingredients

- 2 Cups of boiling water
- 2 Cups of cold water
- 2 Cups of ice
- 4 teabags Earl Gray or Black tea
- 2 1/2 Cups of split strawberries
- 1 lime or lemon
- SPLENDA ZERO™ Liquid Sweetener or regular granulated sugar as need

Instructions

1. brew 2 cups of boiling water and 4 teabags.
2. Add 4 squirts of SPLENDA ZEROTM Liquid Sweetener (or sugar), 2 12 cups of split strawberries, 1 lime or lemon's juice, and crush the strawberries with a fork to release part of the liquid.
3. In a pitcher, mix the steeped tea, strawberries, and 2 cups of chilled water. Stir thoroughly to mix. If necessary, taste and add additional sugar.
4. Pour into a glass, then sip.

167. ICED TEA III

Prep Time: 10 mins

Additional Time: 2 hrs

Total Time: 2 hrs 10 mins

Servings: 16

Ingredients

- 6 black tea bags
- ½ cup of white sugar
- 1 gallon boiling water
- 1 (6 ounce) can refrigerate lemonade concentrate

Directions

1. A 1 gallon glass jar should be filled with sugar and tea bags. Put boiling water inside. Steep at room temperature for two hours. Take out and throw away the tea bags. Add lemonade concentrate and stir. Cool in the refrigerator.

168. SWEET TEA SANGRIA

prep time: 5 MINS

additional time: 8 HOURS

total time: 8 HOURS 5 MINS

Ingredients

- 6 cups of sweet tea
- 1 bottle white wine
- 2 cups of raspberries
- 2 cups of split peveryes
- fresh mint, for garnishing (non-compulsory)

Instructions

2. In a big pitcher, mix wine and sweet tea. Add the fruit and chill for a minimum of two to three hours and preferably eight or more.
3. Serve in elegant cups of with a mint garnish.

169.INSTANT RUSSIAN TEA

Prep Time: 10 mins

Total Time: 10 mins

Servings: 48

Ingredients

- 2 cups of orange-flavor drink powder
- 3 ounces lemonade-flavor drink powder
- ¾ cup of white sugar
- ½ cup of instant tea powder
- ½ tsp ground cinnamon
- ½ tsp ground allspice
- ¼ tsp ground cloves

Directions

1. In a big basin, mix the two drink powders together. Stir in the sugar, tea powder, cinnamon, allspice, and cloves. In three pint-sized jars, divide the mixture.
2. On three gift tags, inscribe the following directions: In a cup of, add 2 to 3 rounded tspfuls and serve with hot water.
3. After adding the gift tags, cap the jars

170.INSTANT SPICED TEA

Prep/Total Time: 10 min.

Ingredients

- 2 cups of orange breakfast drink mix
- 1 cup of unsweetened instant tea
- 1/3 cup of sweetened lemonade drink mix
- 2 tbsp sugar
- 1 tsp ground cinnamon
- 1 tsp ground cloves

Directions

1. Mix all of the ingredients in a big bowl. Use an airtight container for storage.
2. For a single serving: One tbsp of tea mix should be stirred into one cup of hot water until it dissolves.

171.INSTANT SPICED TEA

Prep/Total Time: 10 min.

Ingredients

- 2 cups of orange breakfast drink mix
- 1 cup of unsweetened instant tea
- 1/3 cup of sweetened lemonade drink mix
- 2 tbsp sugar
- 1 tsp ground cinnamon
- 1 tsp ground cloves

Directions

1. All the ingredients should be mixd in a big basin. In a container that is airtight, store.
2. To make one serving: One spoonful of tea mix should be dissolved after one cup of boiling water has been added to a mug.

172.JASMINE HONEY LASSI RECIPE

Ingredients:

- 3 tbsp raw honey
- 1/2 cup of/120 ml warm strong-brewed jasmine tea
- 1 1/2 cups of/255 g diced peveryes
- 3/4 cup of/170 g low-fat greek yogurt
- 4 to 6 ice cubes

Directions:

1. In the hot tea, dissolve the honey. Keep cold in the refrigerator. Blend the peveryes, yogurt, ice, and sweetened tea together in a blender. Once smooth, blend.
2. Provenance: Super-Charged Smoothies: More Than 60 Recipes for Energizing Smoothies written by Sara Corpening Whiteford and Mary Corpening Barber.

173.JASMINE TEA SORBET

INGREDIENTS:

- 1 1/3 cup of sugar
- 3 cups of water
- Zest of 2 organic lemons
- 3 tbs loose Teatulia® jasmine green tea leaves
- 1 cup of freshly squeezed lemon juice (from 4 to 5 lemons)

INSTRUCTIONS:

1. In a medium sauce pan, mix the lemon zest, sugar, and water. Stirring while heating gradually will dissolve sugar. 3 Mins should be spent boiling the mixture. Jasmine tea leaves are added once the heat is turned off. 4 Mins should pass before straining into a large basin. Add the lemon juice and stir. Before freezing, place in the refrigerator to completely chill.

174.JASMINE WHIPPED CREAM

INGREDIENTS

- 1cup of chilled heavy whipping cream
- 1tbsp good quality loose-leaf jasmine tea

- 1tbsp sugar

DIRECTIONS

2. In a bowl, mix cooled cream and tea.
3. Cover and refrigerate for up to two days.
4. Blending bowl after passing cream-tea mixture through a fine filter; discard sediments.
5. Beat while adding sugar until peaks form.

175.CRANBERRY CARDAMOM TEA BREAD

INGREDIENTS

- 5 ounces kumquat gluten-free all-purpose flour
- 4 ounces rolled oats certified gluten free
- 1 tsp baking soda
- 1/2 tsp baking powder
- 1/2 tsp ground cardamom
- 1/4 tsp salt
- 1/2 cup of butter melted
- 1 cup of yogurt
- 2 large eggs
- 2/3 cup of packed brown sugar
- 1 tsp vanilla
- 1/2 cup of dried cranberries
- 1/4 cup of chop up crystallized ginger
- Cooking spray

INSTRUCTIONS

1. In a bowl, mix cooled cream and tea.
2. Cover and refrigerate for up to two days.

3. Blending bowl after passing cream-tea mixture through a fine filter; discard sediments.
4. Beat while adding sugar until peaks form.

176.LAVENDER EARL GREY SCONES

Ingredients

- 2 heaping tsp Earl Grey Lavender tea leaves
- 3 cups of all-purpose flour
- ⅓ cup of sugar
- ½ tsp baking soda
- 2 ½ tsp baking powder
- ¾ tsp kosher salt
- 1 ½ sticks (¾ cups of) unsalted butter, slice into ½ inch pieces
- 1 ¼ cups of buttermilk
- ½ tsp pure vanilla extract
- ¼ cup of heavy cream (for brushing)
- ¼ cup of sugar (for sprinkling)

Instructions

1. Oven: Preheat to 425 degrees.
2. 1 heaping tsp of tea should be steeped for 3 Mins in 1/4 cup of boiling water. Tea should be strained and saved.
3. Grind the last tsp of tea leaves into a very fine powder in a coffee or spice grinder. Add the powder, flour, sugar, baking soda, baking powder, and salt to a sizable mixing basin. Mix everything together.
4. Work the butter into the dry ingredients with thoroughly clean fingertips until the mixture resembles fine breadcrumbs.

5. The buttermilk, vanilla essence, and one tbsp of the brewed tea should be added to the dry ingredients after creating a well in the center. Mix the ingredients until the dry mixture is completely moistened, but do not knead.
6. On a surface dusted with flour, pour the mixture out and gather the dough. Make the dough into a rectangle that is 1 12 inches thick by gently patting it. The scones should be separated into wedges that are approximately 3 12 x 4 inches in size. Place the wedges on a nonstick baking sheet. Don't overwork the dough when lightly gathering the remaining dough to slice out more scones.
7. Every scone's top should be thoroughly brushed with heavy cream before being dusted with sugar.
8. The scones should be baked for 12 Mins, or until just faintly browned. This recipe yields 10 to 12 scones.

177.LEMON BASIL TEA

Prep/Total Time: 10 min.

Ingredients

- 3 quarts water
- 1 cup of thinly split fresh basil leaves
- 1/4 cup of grated lemon zest
- 1/4 cup of English breakfast or other black tea leaves

Directions

1. Bring water to a boil in a big pot. Get rid of the heat. Basil, lemon zest, and tea leaves should also be added. Cover and let steep for 4 Mins. Remove the basil, zest, and tea leaves, then strain. Serve right away.

178.LEMON AND FENNEL ICED TEA

Ingredients

- 4 cups of water
- 1/2 cup of honey or as need
- 1 tbsp fennel seeds
- 4 orange pekoe tea bags
- 3 3- inch long strips of lemon zest yellow part only, removed with a vegetable peeler or paring knife
- 6 tbsp fresh squeezed lemon juice

Instructions

2. Bring to a boil while stirring the water, honey, and fennel seeds in a saucepan. The tea bags and lemon zest strips should be added after taking the pot off the burner. brew for five Mins.
3. Tea should be strained and placed in a heat-resistant pitcher to chill.
4. Lemon juice should be added.
5. Until very cold, chill for at least one hour. If necessary, sweeten the tea more.
6. Serve chilled.

179.LEMON GRAPE COOLERS

Ready In: 10mins

INGREDIENTS

- ice
- 3cups of white grape juice
- 1/2cup of lemon juice
- 2cups of carbonated lemon-lime beverage
- 1bunch grapes, washed and halved
- 1lemon, split into rounds

DIRECTIONS

1. In a large pitcher filled with ice, pour in the grape juice, lemon juice and lemon-lime soda.
2. Gently stir. Add liquid to glasses.
3. Split grapes and lemons are used as a garnish. Enjoy!

180.LEMON ICE TEA MIX

Prep/Total Time: 5 min.

Ingredients

- 7-1/2 cups of sugar
- 2 cups of unsweetened instant tea
- 5 envelopes (.23 ounce every) unsweetened lemonade soft drink mix
- additional ingredients:
- 1 cup of warm water
- Cold water

Directions

1. Mix the sugar, tea, and drink mix in a big bowl. Divide into five equal batches; store in airtight containers in a cool, dry place for up to 6 months. 5 batches with a yield of 8 1/2 cups of overall.
2. Tea preparation: 1-2/3 cups of tea mix should be dissolved in 1 cup of warm water. Put inside a gallon container. 1 gallon of cold water should be added. Add a cover and chill.

181.LEMONADE ICED TEA

Prep: 15 min. + chilling

Ingredients

- 3 quarts water
- 9 tea bags
- 3/4 to 1-1/4 cups of sugar
- 1 can (12 ounces) refrigerate lemonade concentrate, thawed
- Lemon slices, non-compulsory

Directions

1. Bring water to a rolling boil in a Dutch oven. Add tea bags after removing from the heat. For five Mins, cover and steep. Throw away tea bags. Add sugar and lemonade concentrate and stir. Cover and refrigerate until chilled. Serve chilled. Add lemon slices as a garnish if preferred.

182.LEMON ICED TEA

Prep Time: 20 Mins

Cooking Time: 0 Mins

Ingredients

- 8 cups of water, separated
- 6 black tea bags
- ½ cup of granulated sugar
- ¼ cup of fresh squeezed lemon juice

Instructions

2. 4 cups of water should simmer in a pot. Add the tea bags after turning the heat off. Give it five Mins to steep.
3. Once the tea bags are out, add the sugar and stir until it has dissolved. Lemon juice and the remaining 4 cups of cold water should be added to the pan. Chill for about 10 Mins, or until room temperature.
4. Fill a pitcher with the ingredients. at least two hours in the refrigerator before consuming. For up to 4 days, keep.

183.MARMALADE-GLAZED HAM

20 mins preparation

1 hr 20 mins cooking

Ingredients

- Marmalade-glazed ham
- 7 kilogram cooked leg of ham
- 350 gram jar orange marmalade
- 1/4 cup of (55g) brown sugar
- 1/4 cup of (60ml) orange juice
- whole cloves to decorate

Method

1. Ham with marmalade glaze

2. 1Set the oven to 180°C (fan-forced 160°C).
3. 2 Slice a decorative pattern into the rind around 10 cm from the leg's shank end. To remove the rind, run your thumb along the edge just beneath the skin. Start removing the rind from the shank end toward the ham's broadest edge, then discard it.
4. 3 Make shallow slices across the fat with a sharp knife at 3 cm intervals in one direction, then make shallow slices in the other direction to create diamond-shaped slices. Avoid sliceting through top fat since it will separate when cooking.
5. 4 Over a low heat, stir the marmalade, sugar, and juice until the sugar melts.
6. 5
7. Overlapping sheets of baking paper should be used to line a large baking dish (this will make cleaning the dish easier). In a baking dish, place the ham on a wire rack. Apply the marmalade mixture well to the ham, then wrap the shank end with foil.
8. 6
9. Garnish the ham with cloves after 40 Mins of baking. Bake for an additional 40 Mins, or until golden brown all over, baste occasionally with glaze. cold or warm serving.

184.MASALA CHAI

Prep:10 mins

Cook:5 mins

Ingredients

- 200ml-250ml milk (dairy or other)
- 1-2 tbsp sugar or syrup, like stevia, maple syrup, as need
- For the infusion
- 3 green cardamom pods, bashed and husks removed
- ½ cinnamon stick
- 2 cloves
- 3 black peppercorns
- ½ tsp ground ginger
- 2 tsp loose leaf black tea leaves, such as Assam

Method

1. STEP 1 To prepare the infusion, place the cardamom seeds, together with the cinnamon, cloves, and peppercorns, in a pestle and mortar. Blast the ingredients to release the oils; do not create a powder. Pour into a pan and add the ginger and black tea leaves after stirring.
2. STEP 2 Add 400 ml of water, and then gently simmer it over low heat for a few Mins to allow the tea to brew before the water begins to boil. Remove the pan from the heat after adding the milk and sugar or syrup as need. Strain into mugs after 2 Mins of infusion.

185.MATCHA PANNA COTTA

Total Time: 10 Mins

INGREDIENTS

- 1 cup of whole milk
- 2 cups of heavy cream
- 2 tsp gelatin
- 1/2 cup of granulated sugar
- 2 tsp matcha, ceremonial grade
- 2 tsp vanilla
- Toppings (non-compulsory)
- Fresh whipped cream
- Black sesame seed brittle

INSTRUCTIONS

1. Prepare four ramekins by lightly greasing them.
2. Add the gelatin to a cup of after adding half the milk. Stir and let the flower grow.
3. Pour the heavy cream, vanilla, sugar, and matcha powder into a medium saucepan over medium-low heat, and whisk to mix.
4. Add the bloomed gelatin and whisk in the cream mixture.
5. until barely simmering, continue to cook while occasionally whisking.

6. As soon as the cream mixture has reveryed room temperature, divide it among the four ramekins and turn off the heat.
7. Overnight, refrigerate covered ramekins.
8. When ready to serve, submerge every ramekin for five seconds in a bowl of boiling water. Onto a serving platter, invert the ramekin. Sesame brittle and freshly made whipped cream go on top.

186.MATCHA WHITE HOT CHOCOLATE

Prep time 10 mins

Cooking Time 10 mins

Total time20 mins

Ingredients

- ¼ cup of white chocolate chips
- 2 cups of unsweetened almond milk
- 2 tsp AIYA cooking grade matcha
- 1 cup of hot water

Instructions

1. Melt the white chocolate and 1/2 cup of almond milk together. Add the rest of the almond milk after stirring until smooth. Set aside.
2. Matcha should be sifted into a cup of boiling water and whisked until frothy. Pour this into two mugs after stirring it into the almond milk and white chocolate mixture.

3. Make this matcha coconut latte instead if you want a vegan option.

187.MATCHA-COVERED STRAWBERRIES

PREP TIME: 5 Mins

CHILLING TIME: 30 Mins

TOTAL TIME: 35 Mins

Ingredients

- 11 oz white chocolate chips
- 1½ Tbsp matcha powder
- 1 lb California strawberries

Instructions

1. 8 ounces of the white chocolate chips should be melted in the microwave or a double boiler. If melting in the microwave, stir the chocolate between every 30 second interval until the chips are completely melted.
2. Whisk while adding the matcha until it is well integrated.
3. Place every strawberry on a Silpat or parchment-lined baking sheet after being covered in the matcha chocolate. Put the chocolate in the refrigerator for approximately 15 Mins, or until it has firm.

4. Using the same procedure as before, melt the remaining 3 ounces of chocolate chips in a small bowl. Matcha-covered strawberries' bottom tips are dipped in white chocolate before being placed back on the baking sheet. Put until the chocolate shell is firm in the refrigerator.

188.GREEN MANGO SMOOTHIE

Prep time 5 mins

Total time 5 mins

Ingredients

- 2 tsp matcha
- 1 cup of almond milk
- 1 mango, split
- a few handfuls of ice
- non-compulsory - 1 refrigerate banana

Instructions

1. All ingredients should be smoothly mixd. Refrigerate banana should be included for a creamier smoothie.

189.MEZCAL COCKTAIL WITH HIBISCUS AND CILANTRO

Ingredients

- 6 servings
- ½ cup of dried hibiscus flowers
- ½ cup of sugar
- 3 cups of cilantro leaves with tender stems, separated
- ½ cup of mezcal
- ¼ cup of fresh lime juice
- Cilantro flowers or sprigs (for serving)

Preparation

2. Step 1 In a medium saucepan, simmer 3 cups of water. Add hibiscus and turn the heat off. Let soak for 10 Mins. Hibiscus tea should be strained and placed in a basin to cool.
3. Step 2 Simmer 1 cup of water in a little pot. Cook the sugar while stirring until it dissolves. Add 2 cups of cilantro after removing from heat. Steep for 20 Mins. In a small bowl, strain the syrup and allow it to cool.
4. Step 3 In a big pitcher, muddle the remaining 1 cup of cilantro to prepare a cocktail. Stir together the mezcal, lime juice, hibiscus tea, and 1 1/4 cups of cilantro syrup. As the flavor will be muted once you add ice, taste and, if desired, add extra syrup.
5. Step 4: Divide the cocktail among the glasses with ice. Add flowers of cilantro as a garnish.

190.MIGHTY MELON GREEN TEA SMOOTHIE

Prep Time: 10 mins

Total Time: 10 mins

Servings: 2

Ingredients

- 1 cup of brewed green tea (such as Gold Peak®), chilled
- 1 cup of refrigerate pineapple chunks
- 1 cup of cantaloupe chunks
- 1 pear, cored and slice into chunks
- ½ cup of plain Greek yogurt
- 4 fresh mint leaves, or more as need

Direction

1. Blend yogurt, mint leaves, pineapple, cantaloupe, pear, and tea in a food processor. Once smooth, blend.

191.FRESH MINT TEA

Prep:5 mins

Ingredients

- handful of fresh mint (around ½ a pack)
- honey as need

Method

2. STEP 1 Pick up a few mint leaves and quickly clap your other hand over them before dropping the leaves into a teapot or cafetiere. Repeat with the remaining mint, saving a few tiny sprigs for garnishing every glass.
3. STEP 2 Pour boiling water into the pot and let it steep for 2 to 3 Mins, or until the liquid begins to have a faint yellow or green tint. Pour the tea through a strainer into mugs or heatproof glasses, and then add honey as need. If you'd like to garnish the cups of, add the reserved mint there.

192.MINTY TEA PUNCH

Prep: 15 min. + chillin

Ingredients

- 8 cups of water, separated
- 12 mint sprigs
- 4 tea bags
- 1 cup of orange juice
- 1/4 cup of lemon juice
- 1/2 cup of sugar
- Ice cubes
- Orange and lemon slices, non-compulsory

Directions

1. Bring 3 cups of water to a boil in a big pot. Add tea bags and mint after removing from heat. Steep, covered, for 3-5 Mins, depending on preference. Eliminate the tea and mint bags.
2. Add the remaining water, sugar, and the juices of the orange and lemon. Add to a pitcher and chill in the fridge. Slices of orange and lemon may be added if desired.

193.MINT ICED TEA SUMMER COOLER

Prep Time : 5 Mins.

Cooking Time : 5 Mins

Ingredients

- Normal Water - 3 cups of
- Ice water - 2 cups of
- Sugar/Honey - 4 tbsp
- Lemon juice - 3 tbsp
- Tea bag - 1 piece
- Ice cub - 1 cup of
- Fresh mint leaves - 1/2 cup of
- lemon slices - 4

Instructions

1. Pour one cup of water into a container. Bring to a boil after adding sugar.
2. Place the tea bag and a few mint leaves after turning off the heat.
3. Remove the tea bag and mint after five Mins of infusion. Refresh the tea.
4. Add cold water and lemon juice to a container. Add the cooled tea.
5. Four glasses will be filled with a few mint leaves that have been lightly crushed and a few ice cubes.
6. In every glass, pour the lemon-flavored tea.
7. Serve every glass with a slice of lemon.

194.MOM'S RUSSIAN TEA

Prep Time: 5 mins

Cooking Time: 40 mins

Total Time: 45 mins

Servings: 10

Ingredients

- 9 cups of water, separated
- 4 family-size black tea bags (such as Lipton®)
- 1 cup of white sugar
- 1 cup of pineapple juice
- 1 (6 ounce) can refrigerate orange juice concentrate, thawed
- ½ cup of lemon juice
- 6 cloves whole cloves, or more as need
- 2 cinnamon sticks

Directions

1. In a big stockpot, bring 8 cups of water to a boil. Get rid of the heat. Add tea bags and brew for 5–7 Mins. Return the saucepan to medium heat after removing and discarding the teabags.
2. In a another saucepan, heat up 1 cup of water to a boil. Add the sugar and stir until it dissolves. Mixture should be added to the tea stockpot. Lemon juice, orange juice concentrate, and pineapple juice should be added. Stir.
3. Place the tea and juice mixture in the stockpot along with the clove-filled tea ball. Ten Mins of cooking without boiling. Reduce heat to a very low setting and simmer for an additional 15 to 20 Mins to mix flavors.

195.MOM'S TANGERINE ICED TEA

Prep: 10 min. Cook: 5 min. + chilling

Ingredients

- 2-3/4 cups of water, separated
- 4 black tea bags
- 2/3 cup of sugar
- 2 cups of fresh tangerine juice (about 12 tangerines)
- Ice cubes
- Tangerine slices and mint sprigs, non-compulsory

Directions

1. 2 cups of water should be brought to a boil in a small pan. Add tea bags after removing from the heat. For 3 to 5 Mins, steep. Remove tea bags, then slightly chill the tea.
2. Bring remaining water and sugar to a boil in a separate saucepan. Up until the sugar dissolves, cook and stir. Remove from the heat and allow to gently cool.
3. Pour the tea, sugar syrup, and tangerine juice into a large pitcher. Keep cold in the refrigerator.
4. If desired, garnish with mint and tangerine slices and serve over ice.

196. MONEYGUN HOT TODDY

Ingredients

- Makes 1
- 1 tbsp chop up unpeel off fresh ginger
- ½ tsp whole cloves
- 1 tsp loose or 1 bag Darjeeling tea
- ¾ ounce Jamaican black rum
- ¾ ounce cognac
- 1 tbsp honey
- 2 tsp fresh lemon juice
- Lemon wedge (for serving)

Preparation

1. In a measuring glass, muddle the ginger and cloves. Stir for 10 seconds after adding tea and 1 cup of boiling water. Steep for 4 Mins.
2. Warm up a mug by adding hot water to it while you wait. Pour boiling water into mug after tea concoction is finished, then add rum, cognac, and honey. Pour tea into mug after passing through fine-mesh sieve, then swirl to blend. Add the lemon juice, then place the lemon slice inside the mug. Before drinking, let settle for a minute.

197. ORANGE SPICED SWEET TEA

Prep Time 2 Mins

Cooking Time 4 Mins

Servings 1 gallon

Ingredients

- 1 orange peel
- 1 cinnamon stick
- 1 whole clove
- 2 family sized tea bags (to make 1 gallon of tea)
- 4 cups of water
- 1/2 cup of sugar or as need
- 6 cups of ice

Instructions

1. Bring to a boil the water, orange peel, cloves, and cinnamon stick in a pot.
2. After it boils, turn off the heat and add the tea bags.
3. Steep for three to five Mins.
4. Remove the tea bags, cinnamon stick, cloves, and orange peel with a slotted spoon.
5. Add sugar and mix.
6. Six cups of ice should be added to a big pitcher.
7. Stir after adding the tea to the pitcher.
8. Refrigerate
9. Before serving, let the majority of the ice melt.

198.ORANGE TEA

Prep/Total Time: 25 min.

Ingredients

- 7 cup of water
- 1 can (12 ounces) refrigerate orange juice concentrate
- 1/2 cup of sugar
- 2 tbsp lemon juice
- 5 tsp instant tea
- 1 tsp whole clove

Directions

1. Water, orange juice concentrate, sugar, lemon juice, and tea should all be mixd in a big saucepan. Cloves should be tied in a tiny cheesecloth bag and added to the pan. For 15 to 20 Mins, simmer uncovered. Open the spice bag. Serve warm. Refrigerate leftovers in a glass container.

199.ORANGE WARMER

Ingredients

- 6 cups of boiling water
- 6 tsp tea
- 6 cups of orange juice
- 1/2 cup of superfine sugar
- 1 cup of Grand Marnier or Cointreau
- Orange slices, halved
- Whole cloves

Step

2. After adding the boiling water to the tea, steep it for three Mins. Into a punch bowl, strain. Orange juice and sugar should be heated while stirring to dissolve the sugar.

Add to the punch bowl along with the Cointreau or Grand Marnier. Slices of orange adorned with whole cloves are used as a garnish.

3. If preferred, you can heat up a chaffing dish and serve this punch from it.

200.PASSION FRUIT ICED TEA

Prep Time: 5 Mins

Cooking Time: 5 Mins

Total Time: 10 Mins

Servings: 3 people

Ingredients

- 2 1/4 cups of hot water at 175°F
- 3 green tea bags
- 6 passion fruits
- 2 tbsp honey
- ice

Instructions

1. 3 tea bags should be added to 2 1/4 cups of hot, 175°F water. 3–4 Mins, or until desired strength, of brewing. Throw away the tea bags and stir in the honey. Place aside for cooling or refrigeration.

2. Slice open the passion fruit, remove the pulp, and then strain to get the seeds out. To help extract the juice from the passion fruit, use the back of a spoon. About 1/2 cup of passion fruit juice is required.

3. Stir the tea with the juice of the passion fruit. Add ice to serving glasses before adding the passion fruit tea and serving them right away.

Notes

1. If you use loose leaf tea, the beverage will be much more delicious. For flavored tea, I typically use 2 tbsp of loose tea per person.
2. Let the tea cool slightly after brewing if you have a cocktail shaker. Next fill the shaker with a ton of ice, a serving of passion fruit juice, honey, and tea, and shake. Immediately pour the iced tea into a serving glass filled with lots of ice.

201.PEVERY CHILLED SOUP

Prep Time: 10 Mins

Cooking Time: 10 Mins

Chill time: 1 hour

Total Time: 1 hour 20 Mins

Servings: 4 servings

Ingredients

- 3 large fresh peveryes
- 2 cups of pevery mango nectar
- ½ cup of greek vanilla yogurt
- 1 tsp lemon juice
- 1 tsp cinnamon
- 1 tbsp honey

- garnishes of choice (yogurt, fruit, granola)

Instructions

1. Blend all items together in a blender.
2. Spend at least one hour chilling. Serve cold and with the appropriate garnishes.

Notes

1. Information on nutrition does not include garnishes.
2. Pro Tip: Fresh peveryes should feel somewhat soft to the touch, but not mushy, while choosing them. The pevery is not ripe if it is firm. Moreover, search for a pevery with a strong yellow hue.

202.PLUM FENNEL ICED TEA

Ingredients

- Makes about 7 cups of.
- 3 orange pekoe tea bags
- 6 cups of water
- 1 1/2 tbsp fennel seeds
- 4 plums (about 1 pound), pitted and slice into 1/2-inch pieces
- For 1 cup of chilled simple syrup, or as need:
- 1 1/3 cups of sugar
- 1 1/4 cups of water
- Garnish: plum slices

Step

1. In a quart-sized glass measure or a heatproof bowl, place the tea bags.
2. Tea bags are added to 4 cups of water that have just come to a boil in a saucepan. Remove tea bags after 5 Mins of steeping. Tea should be cooled down and chilled for about an hour, covered.
3. Fennel seeds, plums, and the final 2 cups of water are stirred into a pot and brought to a boil for 5 Mins while the tea cools. Press firmly on solids as you strain the mixture through a sieve into a heatproof pitcher. Mixture should be cooled and chilled for about an hour, covered.

4. Add tea and syrup and stir. Tall glasses containing iced tea should be garnished with slices of plum.
5. Creating simple syrup
6. Bring sugar and water to a boil in a pot while stirring; continue boiling until all the sugar has dissolved. Covered, let syrup to cool and chill. A chilled, covered batch of syrup can be prepared two weeks in advance. It yields about 2 cups of.

203.PRUNE SOUFFLES

Preparation time: 30 Mins

Cooking time: 15 Mins

Totaltime: 45 Mins

Ingredients

- 6-6 ounce soufflé molds
  1 tsp sugar
  1 tsp soft butter
  1 cup of pitted prunes
  1 cup of water
  1 tsp Brandy (non-compulsory)
  1 tsp grated lemon rind
  1/2 cup of chop up walnuts, or pecans
  4 egg whites
  1/4 cup of sugar
  1/4 tsp cream of tartar

Preparation

Preheat oven to 375 degrees . Butter the inside of the small soufflé molds. Coat with sugar. Do not touch the inside. In a medium pot, stew the prunes in water, Brandy (non-compulsory), and lemon rind until the moisture is evaporated by half. Purée the prunes in a food processor. Transfer to a medium mixing bowl. Mix in the chop up nuts. Set aside to cool at room temperature. (can be prepared 2 hours in advance up to this point.)

In an electric mixing bowl, whip the egg whites with the cream of tartar. When they revery a soft peaks, gradually add the sugar, and continue beating until the whites are firm and fluffy.

Fold the egg whites into the prune mixture . Fill the mold with the soufflé mixture. Level the soufflé mixture with a spatula. Bake on a baking sheet for 12 to 15 Mins.

Note:

You may also us 1/2 prunes 1/2 dried apricots.

Also, soak prune in tea. Then Armagnac.

204.SWEET RASPBERRY TEA

Ingredients

- 4 quarts water, separated
- 10 tea bags
- 1 package (12 ounces) refrigerate unsweetened raspberries, thawed and undrained
- 1 cup of sugar
- 3 tbsp lime juice

Directions

1. Bring 2 quarts of water to a boil in a saucepan; turn off the heat. Add the tea bags; steep them for 5-8 Mins under cover, as desired. Throw away tea bags.
2. In a large saucepan, mix raspberries, sugar, and the remaining water. Bring to a boil while stirring to dissolve the sugar. Lower heat; let simmer for three Mins, covered. Discard pulp and seeds after pressing mixture through a fine-mesh strainer into a bowl.
3. Mix tea, raspberry syrup, and lime juice in a big pitcher. Refrigerate until chilled, covered.

205.RASPBERRY SWEET TEA

Ingredients

- 4 quarts water, separated
- Sugar substitute equivalent to 1 cup of sugar
- 10 tea bags
- 1 package (12 ounces) refrigerate unsweetened raspberries, thawed and undrained
- 3 tbsp lime juice

Directions

1. Bring 2 qts. of water to a boil in a big pot. Add sugar substitute and stir until it dissolves. Get rid of the heat.
2. Add tea bags and let them steep for 5-8 Mins. Throw away tea bags.
3. Bring the raspberries and remaining water to a boil in a separate pan. Lower heat; allow to simmer for 3 Mins, covered. Remove pulp, then discard it. Add lime and raspberry juices to the tea.
4. Place in a big pitcher. Keep cold in the refrigerator.
5. Nutritional data
6. 17 calories, 0 fat (including 0 saturated fat), 0 cholesterol, 0 sodium, 4g carbohydrate (1g sugars, 1g fiber), and 0 protein are included in 1 cup of.

206.RHUBARB MINT TEA

Ingredients

- 4 cups of chop up fresh or refrigerate rhubarb
- 2 cups of fresh or refrigerate raspberries
- 2 packages (3/4 ounce every) fresh mint leaves
- 3 quarts water
- 4 black tea bags
- 2 cups of sugar
- 12 mint sprigs

Directions

1. Rhubarb, raspberries, mint, and water should all be mixd in a 6-qt stockpot and brought to a boil. Simmer for 30 Mins, uncovered, on low heat. Get rid of the heat. Add the tea bags; steep them for 3-5 Mins under cover, as desired. Tea should be strained through a fine mesh strainer, eliminating pulp and tea bags. Add sugar and stir until it is dissolved. Let it cool. Pour to a pitcher and let cool completely in the fridge. Serve with mint sprigs on top of ice.
2. Nutritional data
3. 1 cup of has 151 calories, 0 fat (0 saturated fat), 0 cholesterol, 3 mg of sodium, 38 grams of carbohydrates (35 grams of sugars, 2 grams of fiber), and 1 gram of protein.

207.RUSSIAN TEA

Prep Time: 10 mins

Total Time: 10 mins

Ingredients

- 2 cups of white sugar
- 2 cups of orange-flavored drink mix (e.g. Tang)
- 1 cup of instant tea powder
- 1 (3 ounce) package powdered lemonade mix
- 2 tsp ground cinnamon
- ½ tsp ground cloves

Directions

1. In a sizable bowl, mix sugar, orange drink mix, tea powder, lemonade powder, ground cinnamon, and ground cloves; stir well. Keep in a container with a tight lid.
2. To provide: 1 cup of hot or cold water should be added to 3 to 4 tbsp of dry mix.
3. Tips
4. If calories are a concern, replace the sugar with a sugar replacement, use an artificially sweetened orange drink mix, and sweeten as need.

208.RUSSIAN TEA (NO MIXES)

Prep Time: 5 mins

Cooking Time: 10 mins

Additional Time: 20 mins

Ingredients

- 1 gallon water, separated
- 4 family-size tea bags
- 2 cups of white sugar
- 1 cinnamon stick
- 1 tsp whole cloves
- 2 cups of pineapple juice
- 2 cups of orange juice
- ¼ cup of lemon juice

Directions

1. In a kettle, boil two quarts of water. After adding the tea bags and removing from the heat, steep for 20 Mins. Take out and throw away the tea bags.
2. In a another pot, mix the remaining 2 quarts of water, the sugar, the cinnamon stick, and the cloves. up to a boil. Add the brewed tea together with the pineapple, orange, and lemon juices.

209.SHEMAKES INSTANT CHAI TEA

Prep Time: 15 mins

Total Time: 15 mins

Ingredients

- 1 ½ cups of instant tea powder
- 2 cups of powdered non-dairy creamer
- ½ cup of dry milk powder
- 1 cup of confectioners' sugar
- ¼ cup of brown sugar
- 1 tsp ground ginger
- 1 tsp ground cinnamon
- 1 tsp ground cloves
- 1 tsp ground cardamom
- 1 tsp ground allspice
- 1 tsp vanilla powder

Directions

1. Mix instant tea, powdered creamer, milk powder, confectioners' sugar, and brown sugar in a food processor. Add vanilla powder, ginger, cinnamon, cloves, cardamom, and other spices. For 2 Mins, process. Use an airtight container for storage.
2. Pour hot water into a mug with 4 tspfuls of the mixture and whisk to mix.

210.SOOTHING HOT GINGER TEA

Prep Time: 5 mins

Cooking Time: 1 mins

Additional Time: 3 mins

Total Time: 9 mins

Ingredients

- 1 (12 fl oz) can ginger ale
- 1 black tea bag

Directions

1. In a mug that can go in the microwave, pour ginger ale. For one to two Mins, reheat in the microwave.
2. For three to five Mins, steep the tea bag in the hot ginger ale.

Cook's Note:

1. If you'd like, you could use diet ginger ale. If you'd prefer, you can use decaffeinated tea or a different taste, like honey vanilla.

211.SPICED CHAI MIX

Ingredients

- 3 cups of nonfat dry milk powder
- 1-1/2 cups of sugar
- 1 cup of unsweetened instant tea
- 3/4 cup of vanilla powdered nondairy creamer
- 1-1/2 tsp ground ginger
- 1-1/2 tsp ground cinnamon
- 1/2 tsp ground cardamom
- 1/2 tsp ground cloves
- non-compulsory garnish:
- Whipped cream

Directions

2. The dry ingredients should be mixd in a food processor and processed until powdery under cover. For up to six months, keep in an airtight container in a cold, dry location.
3. To make one serving: Mix thoroughly and dissolve 3 tsp of the mixture in 3/4 cup of hot water. If using, top with whipped cream.

Nutrition Facts

1. 1g fat (1g saturated fat), 3mg cholesterol, 75mg sodium, 21g carbohydrate (19g sugars, 0 fiber), 5g protein are all contained in 3 tbsp, which have 114 calories. Exchanges for diabetics: 1 1/2 starch.

212.HOT SPICED GREEN TEA

Ingredients

- 2 cinnamon sticks (3 inches)
- 4 green tea bags
- 1/2 tsp chop up fresh gingerroot
- 1/2 tsp grated lemon zest
- 4 cardamom pods, crushed
- 4 cups of boiling water
- 2 tbsp honey

Directions

2. Mix the first five ingredients in a big bowl. Add some hot water. For 5–6 Mins, cover and steep. Discard tea bags and spices after straining. Tea with honey in it. Serve right away.
3. Nutritional data
4. 33 calories, 0 fat (0 saturated fat), 0 cholesterol, 0 sodium, 9g of carbohydrates (0 fiber, 0 sugars), and 0 protein are included in 1 cup of. Exchanges for diabetics: 1/2 starch.

213.SPICED ICED TEA

Ingredients

- 4 cups of boiling water
- 4 tea bags
- 1 cinnamon sticks (3 inches)
- 4 whole cloves
- Sugar substitute equivalent to 4 tsp sugar
- Ice cubes, fresh mint and lemon slices

Directions

1. Put a heat-resistant pitcher in the boiling water. Tea will steep for 15 Mins after you've added the tea bags, cinnamon, cloves, and sugar alternative.
2. Tea bags, cinnamon, and cloves should all be discarded. Tea should be poured over ice in glasses and topped with lemon and mint.

214.SPICED MILK TEA : MASALA CHAI

INGREDIENTS

- CHAI
- 2cups of liquid milk
- 2cups of water
- 6tsp sugar
- 3tsp dried tea leaves (Assam is recommended)
- 1/2tsp masala, spice
- MASALA MIX
- 1/2cup of ground ginger

- 1/8cup of clove
- 1/3cup of whole black peppercorn
- 3tbsp cinnamon, ground
- 1tsp grated nutmeg, around 1/4 piece
- 2tbsp green cardamom pods

DIRECTIONS

1. Blend or ground all the components for the masala combination in a spice grinder. Only a small amount of this combination will be needed; the rest can be kept in an airtight container.
2. Place the milk in a pot with 2 cups of water, and then heat to a boil.
3. Add the masala, sugar, and tea leaves. Stir the mixture until it becomes dark (8 Mins).
4. Turn off the heat, pour into cups of, and serve immediately.

215.SPICY MINT TEA

INGREDIENTS

- 1orange pekoe tea bag
- 6large mint sprigs, large stems with large leaves (lightly crushed)
- 1/4tsp cayenne pepper
- 2cups of boiling water, boiling
- 1cup of white sugar, white
- 1/2cup of lemon juice, fresh squeezed
- 1cinnamon stick
- 2slices lemons, garnish
- 2mint sprigs, garnish

DIRECTIONS

1. With 2 cups of boiling water, steep 1 tea bag, 6 mint stems, and cayenne pepper.

2. Remove the liquid only after straining the mixture.
3. Refrigerate after adding sugar, lemon juice, and a cinnamon stick to the mint mixture.
4. Remove the cinnamon stick and add equal parts of water to the mint mixture before serving.
5. Pour over ice in a large glass, garnished with a lemon slice and a fresh mint sprig.

216.SPICY MINT TEA

Ingredients

- 6 cups of water
- 2 cinnamon sticks
- 4 whole cloves
- 4 whole allspice
- 2 cups of fresh mint leaves
- Honey, non-compulsory

Directions

1. Water, cinnamon, cloves, and allspice are brought to a boil. for one minute, boil. Add mint leaves and stir. After 5 Mins, remove from heat and steep. Filter into cups of. If desired, add honey to sweeten.

217.THAI PEANUT DRESSING

PREP TIME5 mins

TOTAL TIME5 mins

ngredients

- 1/4 cup of creamy peanut butter (see note 1)
- 3 tbsp rice vinegar (see note 2)
- 2 tbsp soy sauce
- 2 tbsp honey (see note 3)
- 2 tbsp lime juice (from 1 lime)
- 1 tbsp fresh ginger chop up
- 1 tsp sesame oil
- 2 cloves garlic chop up
- 1/4 tsp red chili flakes
- Salt and freshly ground black pepper

Instructions

1. Peanut butter, rice vinegar, soy sauce, honey, lime juice, ginger, sesame oil, garlic, and red pepper flakes should all be mixd in a small bowl. Add salt and pepper as need (I like 1 tsp salt and 1/2 tsp pepper). Thin the dressing with water, 1 tsp at a time, if it is too thick.

218.STRAWBERRIES AND CHAMOMILE MINT CREAM

Prep Time: 25 Mins

Rest and chill time: 10 hours

Total Time: 10 hours 25 Mins

Ingredients

- Infused Whipped Cream
- 1 pint heavy whipping cream
- 4 tbsp chamomile flowers loose tea
- 2 tbsp powdered sugar
- Macerated Strawberries
- 16 ounces strawberries
- 1 tbsp granulated sugar
- Base and Topping
- 8 graham crackers

Instructions

2. Recipe for Infused Whipped Cream
3. Put whipping cream in a bowl made of glass or metal. Flowers from chamomile are included in.
4. Bowl should be covered and put in the fridge. For 8 to 12 hours, let sit.
5. To get the most cream, pour the cream through a sieve and scrape it with a rubber spatula. Toss the chamomile blossoms away.
6. Put cream and powdered sugar in the mixer's bowl. Cream should be whisked using the whisk attachment at medium speed until peaks form.
7. Recipe for Macerated Strawberries
8. Slice, transport, dry, and clean strawberries. Put the strawberries in a glass bowl, add the sugar, and mix to evenly coat.
9. For at least two hours, but preferably overnight, cover the bowl and put it in the fridge.
10. How to Assemble Strawberries and Chamomile Cream
11. Graham crackers should be placed in a bowl and crushed with a spoon. Make medium-sized to tiny crumbles (you can also use a blender or processor).
12. A graham cracker base, macerated strawberries (and juice), and infused whipped cream are placed in dessert cups of or bowls. Then, sprinkle some more berries, graham cracker crumbs, and mint on top.
13. Dispense and savor!

Notes

1. Ahead of time: It could be a good idea to begin preparing these the previous day. Strawberries and heavy whipping cream can be prepared the night before or the next morning. The next day, this will be simpler as a result.

2. Substitutions: You may certainly use ready-made whipped cream and other shortbread-style cookies for the graham crackers.

219.SUGAR-FREE RUSSIAN TEA

Ingredients

- 4-1/2 tsp sugar-free orange drink mix
- 3-1/2 tsp Crystal Light lemonade drink mix
- Artificial sweetener equivalent to 16 tsp sugar
- 1 tsp ground cinnamon
- 1/2 tsp ground cloves

Directions

1. Mix all items together thoroughly. Use an airtight container for storage. Stir well after adding 1/4 tsp of the mixture to 3/4 cup of hot water to make one serving.

220.SUMMERTIME FRUIT TEA

Ingredients

- 12 cups of water, separated
- 1-1/2 cups of sugar
- 9 tea bags
- 1 can (12 ounces) refrigerate lemonade concentrate, thawed
- 1 can (12 ounces) refrigerate pineapple-orange juice concentrate, thawed

Directions

1. Boil 4 cups of water in a Dutch oven. Add sugar and mix until it dissolves. Add tea bags after removing from the heat. For 5-8 Mins, steep. Throw away tea bags. Mix in the remaining water and juice concentrates. Serve chilled.

Ingredients

- 1 can (12 ounces) refrigerate pink lemonade concentrate, thawed, undiluted
- 1 package (20 ounces) refrigerate unsweetened strawberries, partially thawed
- 1/4 cup of sugar
- 2 cups of cold brewed strong tea
- 2 liters ginger ale, chilled
- Ice cubes

Directions

2. Mix sugar, strawberries, and lemonade concentrate in a food processor. Process while covered until smooth. Add tea and transfer to a big pitcher or punch bowl. Ice cubes and ginger ale should be added. Serve right away.

Nutrition Facts

3. 32g of carbohydrates (29g sugars, 1g fiber), 0 protein, 122 calories, 0 fat (0 saturated fat), 0 cholesterol, and 13mg of sodium in 1 cup of.

222.SWEET PEVERY ICED TEA

-
  4 cups of water + more to top up
- ½ cup of granulated sugar
- ½ tsp baking soda
- 8 tea bags black tea
- 1 cup of pevery nectar
- 5 fresh peveryes split
- Cook ModePrevent your screen from going dark

Instructions

4. 4 cups of water should come to a boil.
5. Mix the boiling water, baking soda, and sugar in a sizable, heat-resistant pitcher or jug to completely dissolve the sugar. After adding the tea bags, steep them for 10 Mins.
6. Get rid of the tea bags.
7. Pour the pevery nectar, then pour cold water into the remaining space in the pitcher or jug. Keep cold in the refrigerator.
8. Tall glasses should be filled with ice, pevery slices, and tea before being served.

223.SWEET RASPBERRY TEA

Ingredients

- 4 quarts water, separated
- 10 tea bags
- 1 package (12 ounces) refrigerate unsweetened raspberries, thawed and undrained
- 1 cup of sugar
- 3 tbsp lime juice

Directions

1. Bring 2 quarts of water to a boil in a saucepan; turn off the heat. Add the tea bags; steep them for 5-8 Mins under cover, as desired. Throw away tea bags.
2. In a large saucepan, mix raspberries, sugar, and the remaining water. Bring to a boil while stirring to dissolve the sugar. Lower heat; let simmer for three Mins, covered. Discard pulp and seeds after pressing mixture through a fine-mesh strainer into a bowl.
3. Mix tea, raspberry syrup, and lime juice in a big pitcher. Refrigerate until chilled, covered.

Nutrition Facts

1. A cup of has 66 calories, 0 fat (0 saturated fat), 0 cholesterol, 5 mg of sodium, 17 grams of carbs, and 0 grams of protein.

224.SWEET TEA CONCENTRATE

Ingredients

- 2 medium lemons
- 4 cups of sugar
- 4 cups of water
- 1-1/2 cups of English breakfast tea leaves or 20 black tea bags
- every serving:
- 1 cup of cold water
- Ice cubes

Directions

2. Peel the lemon lengthwise into strips using a sharp paring knife or vegetable peeler, reserving only the zest. Fruit should be squeezed, with a 1/3 cup of juice set aside for later use.
3. Sugar and water should be mixd in a big sauce pan. Over medium heat, bring to a boil. Lower heat; cover and simmer for 3 to 5 Mins, stirring periodically, until sugar dissolves. Add the tea and lemon zest after turning off the heat. 15 Mins of steeping under cover. Tea leaves and lemon zest should be removed before straining; add lemon juice after. Till room temperature, cool.
4. Move the container to one that has a tight-fitting lid. Keep in the fridge for up to two weeks.
5. Tea preparation: Mix 1 cup of cold water and 1/4 cup of concentrate in a large glass with ice.

225.TEA PUNCH

Prep Time: 30 mins

Additional Time: 4 hrs

Total Time: 4 hrs 30 mins

Ingredients

- 1 cup of white sugar
- 1 cup of strong brewed black tea
- 4 cups of orange juice
- 4 cups of pineapple juice
- 4 cups of prepared lemonade
- 1 (2 liter) bottle ginger ale, chilled

Directions

1. Mix tea and sugar in a pitcher. Mix the sugar until it dissolves. Add lemonade, orange juice, and pineapple juice after stirring. 4 hours of refrigeration are required.
2. Pour the cold juice mixture into a punch bowl just before serving, then stir in the ginger ale.

226.TEA SMOKED DUCK

Prep Time20 mins

Cooking Time40 mins

Ingredients

- 4 to 6 skin-on duck breasts
- DRY RUB
- 2 tbsp kosher salt
- 1 tbsp Sichuan peppercorns
- 2 tsp black peppercorns
- 1/4 tsp Insta Cure No. 1 (non-compulsory)
- 2 tbsp Shaoxing wine or dry sherry
- SMOKING INGREDIENTS
- 1/2 cup of rice
- 1/2 cup of loose-leaf tea
- 1/2 cup of firmly packed brown sugar
- 1 star anise pod (non-compulsory)
- 1 tsp dried orange or tangerine peel (non-compulsory)
- TO FINISH
- 2 tsp peanut or other vegetable oil
- 1 tsp toasted sesame oil
- 8 ounces mushrooms, split
- 8 ounces bok choy, coarsely chop up
- 1 tbsp peel off and chop up fresh ginger
- 1 tbsp sugar
- 1 tbsp soy sauce

- 1/3 cup of duck stock or chicken stock
- 2 to 4 fresh hot red chiles, thinly split

Instructions

1. Duck breasts should be taken out of the fridge. Kosher salt, Sichuan peppercorns, black peppercorns, and curing salt should be mixed together and ground into a powder in a spice grinder or in a mortar and pestle to form the dry rub. The spice mixture should be applied after evenly moistening the duck breasts with the wine. Every breast should be separately wrapped in plastic wrap before being placed in the refrigerator to cure for at least 4 hours and ideally 12 hours. Let huge breasts to cure for 24 hours if using them (see headnote).
2. After the breasts have fully cured, rinse the cure from them and pat them dry. On a cooling rack, place them skin side up and let dry for two to three hours. If possible, point a fan towards the duck to ensure thorough drying.
3. A wok should be lined with aluminum foil so that it extends 2 inches past the rim on all sides. This will serve as the seal for the wok. Add a rack to the bottom of the wok after placing all of the smoking ingredients there (or use 4 cheap chopsticks or wooden skewers to improvise a rack). Lay the duck on the rack with the skin side up. After sealing it, place the wok on the heat. If you're using only foil, spread it out over the wok's top and crimp the edges. If you have a lid, close it and seal everything with the extra foil covering the wok. Make sure the stove exhaust fan is turned up high. (You might want to take into account doing this outside on the grill if your exhaust fan is not too powerful.)
4. For 3 to 5 Mins, increase the heat to high, and wait until the smoking materials barely start to smoke. There will be a lot of popping, snapping, and crackling. For 20 to 30 Mins, smoke the duck over medium heat. Duck breasts of average size will require 20 Mins, but extremely huge ones like Moulard or goose breasts will require the entire 30 Mins.
5. Take the cover off and the duck breasts will come out. At this point, you can let them to cool and put them in the refrigerator for a day or two. To finish them, heat the 2 tsp of vegetable oil in a sauté pan over medium-high heat [[the amount you call out isn't possible because in the ingredient list you have 2 tsp]]. Cook the breasts until the skin is crisp by adding them with the skin side down. The meat side will already be done; avoid cooking it. While the vegetables cook, remove the breasts from the pan, slice them, and set them aside.
6. In the same skillet you used to fry the duck skin, increase the heat to high to sauté the vegetables. With the remaining oil in the pan, add the mushrooms and stir to

coat. As soon as the mushrooms start to release their water, let them sit undisturbed for 2 to 4 Mins. The bok choy, ginger, and tsp of sesame oil should all be added at this point and stir-fried for 1 minute.

7. Toss in the stock, soy sauce, and sugar after adding them. This should be quickly boiled for 4 Mins to allow the liquid to thicken. After removing the pan from the heat, stir in the chilies and duck slices before serving. Serve right away.

227. THAI TEA CAKE WITH CONDENSED MILK CUSTARD SAUCE RECIPE

Active:30 mins

Total:75 mins

Serves:12 servings

Ingredients

- Save Recipe
- 2 cups of whole milk, room temperature, separated
- 2 tbsp unsweetened loose Thai tea leaves
- 8 tbsp (1 stick) unsalted butter, softened
- 1 1/2 cups of (about 10 1/2 ounces) granulated sugar
- 3 large eggs, room temperature
- 2 1/4 cups of (about 11 1/2 ounces) all-purpose flour
- 1/2 tsp salt
- 2 tsp baking powder
- 6 large egg yolks
- 1 (14-ounce) can sweetened condensed milk

Directions

1. In a heat-resistant dish or glass measuring cup of, add 1 1/4 cups of milk. Microwave for 30 seconds or until warm. Tea leaves are added; set aside.
2. Set aside. Oil a 10-inch springform pan or a 13-by-9-by-2-inch pan, and cover the bottom with parchment paper. Set the oven to 350° F.
3. Flour, salt, and baking powder should be mixd in a medium bowl; set aside. For about 30 seconds, whip butter in a sizable mixing basin with an electric mixer set to medium speed. While beating the mixture and scraping down the bowl's sides as necessary, gradually add sugar, 1/4 cup of at a time.
4. One at a time, beat the eggs into the butter mixture, adding them one at a time, for a total of about a minute.
5. Pour tea-infused milk through a strainer with fine mesh. Fold the flour combination and the tea-infused milk into the butter mixture alternating using a rubber spatula. Spread the batter onto the prepared pan once it has been thoroughly mixed, and bake for 30 to 35 Mins, or until a toothpick inserted in the center comes out clean. Cake should be taken out of the oven and allowed to cool in the pan.
6. While waiting, prepare the custard sauce by whisking together the remaining milk and condensed milk in a 1-quart heavy-bottomed pot or saucier. In a medium mixing bowl, add the egg yolks and whisk to mix.
7. Remove the pot from the heat as soon as the condensed milk mixture begins to boil. Pour a thin stream of boiling milk into the yolks while carefully pouring them in with one hand. Using the other hand, vigorously whisk the mixture to ensure that everything is well mixd.
8. Refill the milk pot with the egg mixture, whisking continually while it cooks on low heat. The custard sauce will thicken in under a minute. Turn off the heat, strain the custard through a fine-mesh strainer into a serving bowl with a spout if possible, and keep warm under a cover. (The total amount of sauce should be around 2 1/2 cups of.)
9. Together with the warm custard sauce, serve the cake. (Thin the sauce with a little warm milk if it gets too thick after standing.)

228. TOUCH-OF-MINT ICED TEA

Ingredients

- 6 cups of boiling water
- 4 tea bags
- 1 cup of packed fresh mint
- 3/4 cup of refrigerate lemonade concentrate
- Ice cubes

Directions

1. Pour boiling water over tea bags in a heat-resistant basin or pitcher; cover and steep for 5 Mins. Remove the tea bags. 15 Mins to cool. 5. Add mint and let it steep. Strain. Stir in the lemonade concentrate thoroughly. Refrigerate. Pour over ice and, if wanted, garnish with mint and lemon.

229. VANILLA CHAI TEA

Ingredients

- 8 whole peppercorns
- 1/2 tsp whole allspice
- 2 cardamom pods
- 1 cinnamon stick (3 inches)
- 4 whole cloves
- 8 tea bags
- 1 tbsp honey
- 4 cups of boiling water
- 2 cups of 2% milk

- 1 tbsp vanilla extract
- 1/2 cup of heavy whipping cream
- 1-1/2 tsp confectioners' sugar
- Ground allspice

Directions

2. The first five ingredients should be put in a big basin. Crush the mixture with the wooden spoon handle's tip until the scents are released. Tea bags, honey, and boiling water are added. Covered steeping time is 6 Mins.
3. Milk should be heated in a small pan. Pour the tea, milk, and vanilla into a heatproof pitcher. Drain the tea.
4. Cream should be beaten in a small bowl until it starts to thicken. As soft peaks start to form, add confectioners' sugar and beat. Add some allspice and whipped cream to the portions.
5. Whipped cream can be prepared a few hours ahead of time; simply cover and chill.

Nutrition Facts

1. 131 calories, 9g fat (6g saturated fat), 33mg cholesterol, 48mg sodium, 9g carb (7g sugars, 0 fiber), and 3g protein are contained in 1 cup of (with 2-1/2 tsp topping).

230.HOW TO MAKE VEGAN KETO CHAI TEA LATTE

Preparation:5 Mins

Cooking:25 Mins

Total:30 Mins

Ingredients

- 2cups ofwater
- 2black tea bags

- 1tspground cinnamon,separated
- ½tspvanilla extract
- 2cardamom pods
- pinchground allspice
- pinchground ginger
- pinchground nutmeg
- pinchground cloves
- pinchsalt
- ½cup ofalmond milk
- ½tsperythritol

Instructions

2. Over medium heat, bring a small pot of water to a boil. Add the tea bags together with the salt, vanilla extract, cardamom, ginger, nutmeg, cloves, and 12 tsp of cinnamon.
3. For 20 Mins, simmer. Remove tea bags, then filter the liquid.
4. In a saucepan over medium heat, warm the almond milk containing the erythritol.
5. Divide mixture between 2 mugs after adding tea. On top, add the remaining cinnamon.
6. Dispense and savor!

231.VERY BERRY TEA SMOOTHIE

Prep Time: 10 mins

Total Time: 10 mins

Ingredients

- 1 cup of brewed black tea (such as Gold Peak®), chilled
- 1 cup of refrigerate mixed berries
- 1 cup of refrigerate pineapple chunks
- 1 banana, broken into chunks and refrigerate
- ½ lemon, juiced

- 3 fresh mint leaves, or more as need
- 1 tsp honey (Non-compulsory)

Directions

1. Blend tea with the berries, pineapple, banana, mint, lemon juice, and honey. Once smooth, blend.

232.VICTORIAN FARMHOUSE ICED TEA

INGREDIENTS

- 4individual tea bags
- 4cups of boiling water
- 1(12 ounce) can refrigerate raspberry-cranberry refrigerate juice concentrate (thawed)
- 4cups of cold water
- ice cubes or ice ring

DIRECTIONS

2. Teabags should be placed in a large measuring cup of, covered with boiling water, and steeped for 5 Mins before being removed.
3. In a covered container, chill.
4. AT SERVING TIME: In a 2 quart serving pitcher, mix the juice and cold water; add the tea; and stir.
5. SERVING SUGGESTIONS: Pour into a punch bowl with an ice ring or serve over ice cubes.
6. Oh my goodness, this is simply too much!

Ingredients

- 6 cardamom pods
- 1/2 tsp whole peppercorns
- 5 cups of water
- 1/4 cup of honey
- 2 cinnamon sticks (3 inches)
- 8 whole cloves
- 3 whole star anise
- 1 tbsp chop up fresh gingerroot
- 5 black tea bags
- 2 cups of whole milk
- 1 tbsp vanilla extract
- Ground nutmeg, non-compulsory

Directions

1. Cardamom pods and peppercorns should be mixd and ground in a spice grinder or using a mortar and pestle until flavors are released.
2. Bring water to a boil in a big pot. Simmer for five Mins or as need after adding the cardamom combination, honey, cinnamon sticks, cloves, star anise, and ginger. Get rid of the heat. tea bags; cover and steep for five Mins.
3. Milk is being heated in a small pan in the meantime. Discard spices and tea bags after straining the tea. Add vanilla and boiling milk and stir. Into mugs, pour. Sprinkle with nutmeg, if preferred.
4. Nutritional data
5. 1 cup of has 102 calories, 3g of fat (2g of which are saturated), 8mg of cholesterol, 44mg of salt, 16g of carbohydrates, and 3g of protein.

234. WINTER HERB TEA MIX

Ingredients

- 6 tbsp dried mint
- 1 tbsp dried sage leaves
- 1 tbsp dried rosemary, crushed
- 1 tbsp dried thyme
- additional ingredients (for every serving):
- 1 cup of boiling water
- 1 tsp honey
- 1 lemon wedge

Directions

1. The herbs should be mixd in a tiny sealed container. For up to 6 months, store in a cool, dry location.
2. Tea preparation: In a glass measuring cup of, add 1-and-a-half tsp of tea mix. Crush the mixture using the end of a wooden spoon handle until scents are released. Add some hot water. For ten Mins, cover and steep. Discarding the herbs, strain the tea into a mug. Serve with lemon after adding honey.

Nutrition Facts

1. 27 calories, 0 fat (0 saturated fat), 0 cholesterol, 2 mg of sodium, 7g of carbohydrates (6g sugars, 1g fiber), and 0g of protein are included in 1 cup of hot tea.

235.HOT TEA PUNCH

Ingredients

- Makes about 6 cups of
- 6 cups of water
- 3/4 cup of sugar
- 2 cinnamon sticks
- 8 whole cloves
- 5 tea bags
- 1 1/2 cups of orange juice
- 1/3 cup of fresh lemon juice
2. Bring first 4 ingredients to boil in heavy large saucepan over high heat, stirring until sugar dissolves. Boil 6 Mins. Remove from heat. Add tea bags. Cover and let steep 10 Mins. Discard tea bags. Add orange and lemon juices to punch. (Can be prepared 1 day ahead. Cover and refrigerate. Rewarm before continuing.) Using slotted spoon, remove whole spices. Serve hot.

236.WARM MILK PUNCH WITH INDIAN SPICES

Ingredients

- 4 cups of water
- 8 whole cloves
- 4 whole cardamom pods
- 1 tsp fennel seeds
- 1 cinnamon stick
- 1 1/4-inch thick slice fresh ginger
- 3 bags Darjeeling tea or 3 tbsp Darjeeling tea leaves
- 1 cup of low-fat milk
- 1/4 cup of sugar
- 4 3x1/2-inch strips orange peel

- Additional cinnamon sticks (non-compulsory)

Step

3. In a medium saucepan, mix the first 6 ingredients and bring to a boil. Lower the heat to low, cover the pot, and simmer for 10 Mins. Remove the pan from the heat, then add the tea bags or leaves. Cover the pan and steep the mixture for 30 Mins.
4. Put liquid in another pot after straining. Tea can be given milk and sugar. Stirring as it simmers will cause the sugar to dissolve. Pour punch into four glasses. If desired, garnish with more cinnamon sticks and orange peel strips.

237.WAKE COUNTY COOLER

Ingredients

- 12 Servings
- 1 750-ml bottle vodka
- ⅔ cup of loose-leaf black tea
- ¼ cup of sugar
- ½ ounce fresh lemon juice
- Club soda
- Lemon wedges (for garnish)
- Mint sprigs (for garnish)

Preparation

1. In a big pitcher, mix vodka and tea. Let to stand for two hours at room temperature, stirring occasionally. Into a different big pitcher, strain. Shake a container with the sugar and 1/4 cup of water until the sugar is dissolved, then pour the mixture into the vodka. Put ice in a Collins glass for every cooler. Add 2 oz. of flavored vodka and lemon juice. Add club soda on top, then add a lemon wedge and a mint sprig as garnish.

Nutrition Per Serving

2. 12 portions

3. Every dish has: Calories (kcal) 150 g of fat, 0 g of saturated fat, 0 mg of cholesterol, and 0 g of carbohydrates (g) 4 Food Fiber (g) Total Sugars = 0 (g) 3 g of protein with no sodium (mg) 0

238.ULTIMATE HYDRA

Ingredients

- Makes 2 (12-ounce) glasses
- 2 cups of (500 ml) green tea, refrigerate in ice-cube trays
- 12 grapes
- 1 tbsp honey
- 1 small handful mint
- Juice of 1 lime
- 1 1/4 cups of (300 ml) coconut water
- 1/2 Lebanese cucumber (or 1/4 English cucumber), split
- 1 tbsp chia seeds
- 1 tsp aloe vera juice

Step

1. In a jug, mix the cucumber, grapes, honey, mint, lime juice, coconut water, and green tea ice cubes. Stir well. Stir in the aloe vera and chia seeds. Ten Mins should pass so the mixture can thicken.

239.TROPICAL TEA

Prep10 Min

Total10 Min

Servings12

Ingredients

- 4 1/2cups of water
- 4cups of iced tea
- 1can (12 ounces) refrigerate pineapple-orange juice concentrate, thawed
- Fresh mint leaf, if desired

Steps

2. 1 In a big pitcher, mix water, iced tea, and juice concentrate.
3. 2 Put the food on ice. Mint is a good garnish.

240.TROPICAL STEVIA ICED GREEN TEA

TimePrep: 10 mins

CaloriesTotal: 15

-
  2 cups of hot water
- 2 tropical green tea bags
- 1 ounce lemon juice
- 1/2 ounce orange juice

- 2 packets Wholesome Organic Stevia, or more as need
- Ice
- 2 cups of hot water
- 2 tropical green tea bags
- 1 ounce lemon juice
- 1/2 ounce orange juice
- 2 packets Wholesome Organic Stevia, or more as need
- Ice

Directions

1. heated water is used to make tropical tea. Once well steeped, remove tea bags.
2. Add Wholesome Organic Stevia, lemon juice, and orange juice.
3. Add ice and allow to chill.

241.TOUCH-OF-MINT ICED TEA

Ingredients

- 6 cups of boiling water
- 4 tea bags
- 1 cup of packed fresh mint
- 3/4 cup of refrigerate lemonade concentrate
- Ice cubes
- Lemon slices and additional mint, non-compulsory

Directions

1. Pour boiling water over tea bags in a heat-resistant basin or pitcher; cover and steep for 5 Mins. Remove the tea bags. 15 Mins to cool. 5. Add mint and let it steep. Strain. Stir in the lemonade concentrate thoroughly. Refrigerate. Pour over ice and, if wanted, garnish with mint and lemon.

242. TIPSY TEA WITH HOMEMADE SWEET TEA

Ingredients

- Serves 1
- 2 ounces orange-flavored vodka, chilled
- 6 ounces Sweet Tea , chilled
- Garnish:
- 1/2 orange wheel (non-compulsory)

Add the vodka and tea to a tall glass filled with ice; stir well. Garnish, if desired.

243. TEA-AND-LEMON GRAVY

Ingredients

- Makes 3 1/2 cups of Servings
- 8 cups of low-salt chicken broth
- 2 celery stalks, coarsely chop up
- 2 carrots, peel off, coarsely chop up
- 1 medium onion, halved
- 1 fresh rosemary sprig
- Neck, heart, and gizzard, reserved from 22-pound turkey 1
- Lemon
- 1 Earl Grey tea bag
- 5 tbsp butter
- 5 tbsp flour
- 1/2 cup of whipping cream
- 1tbsp lightly grated lemon peel

Preparation

2. Step 1 Mix the first six ingredients in a big pot. Peel a lemon with a vegetable peeler (yellow part only). To the broth mixture, add peel. Mixture should be brought to a boil before being simmered for 45 Mins or until the neck and gizzard are soft.
3. Step 2 Take the neck, heart, and gizzard out of the broth and coarsely chop them. Grab the meat from the neck and slice. Sort the broth. Bring back the broth to the pan and cook for 10 Mins to reduce it to 3 cups of. Tea bag added after heat is removed. For 10 Mins, cover and steep. Delete the tea bag.
4. Step 3: Melt butter over medium heat in a heavy medium saucepan. Mix in the flour. Sauté for about 5 Mins, stirring frequently, until light brown. Cream and broth are whisked in. Bring to a boil; lower heat to medium; and simmer for 8 Mins, stirring often, until just slightly thickened and smooth. Add the grated peel and the pieces of the neck, heart, and gizzard. Add salt and pepper as need.

244. TEA GRANITA WITH ROSE WATER AND BAKLAVA

Ingredients

- Makes 4 to 6 servings
- 5 cups of bottled water
- 3/4 cup of sugar
- 1 tsp rose water*
- 6 tea bags (preferably black tea)
- 3/4 cup of half and half
- Organic rose petals (non-compulsory)
- Purchased baklava

Step

1. In a big pitcher, mix 5 cups of water, sugar, and rose water until the sugar dissolves. Pushing to fully submerge, add tea bags. Place on a sunny windowsill while covered with foil. Steep for at least three hours, or until the tea is dark.
2. Take out and discard the tea bags. Tea with half and half mixd. Fill the 13x9x2 inch glass dish with the ingredients. About an hour of freezing is required to revery the margins. In a dish, roughly chop the ingredients. Freeze for about a more hour, or practically solid.
3. Transfer the granita to the processor in two batches and process until smooth. Once more, freeze the same dish for an hour. One more time, mix the two batches again. 1 hour of freezing
4. Granita in the dish should be broken up into flakes with a fork. Wrap; then freeze.
5. Plan ahead: made a day in advance.
6. Place granita in serving bowls and, if wanted, garnish with rose petals. Serve baklava and granita.

245. TEA BREAD WITH VINE FRUIT AND PINE NUTS

Ingredients

- Makes 8 servings
- 1 1/2 cups of water
- 6 tsp black tea leaves or 6 tea bags (such as orange pekoe)
- 1/2 cup of golden raisins
- 1/2 cup of dried currants
- 1 1/4 cups of self-rising flour
- 1/4 cup of sugar
- 1 tsp baking powder
- 1/4 cup of light corn syrup
- 1 large egg
- 2 tsp vanilla extract
- 1 1/4 cups of pine nuts, lightly toasted

Step

1. In a small saucepan, bring 1 1/2 cups of water to a boil. Including tea leaves. Get rid of the heat. 15 Mins of steeping time under cover.
2. Put the tea leaves in a small basin and strain the tea. Add the currants and raisins and soak for 45 Mins. Remove soaking liquid from the raisin mixture and set aside the raisin mixture and 3/4 cup of the soaking liquid separately. Any liquid that is left over should be discarded.
3. Set the oven to 325 F. Metal loaf pan, 8 1/2x 4 1/2x 2 1/2 inches, butter and flour. In a medium bowl with the flour, sugar, and baking powder. Add the egg, vanilla, corn syrup, and 3/4 cup of the saved soaking liquid. By using an electric mixer, mix ingredients thoroughly. Add pine nuts and the mixture of raisins. Pour batter into pan and level the top.
4. Bake bread for about 55 Mins, or until it is deeply brown and a tester put into the center comes out clean. 15 Mins to cool in the pan. Rotate the bread onto the rack. Complete cooling. (May be made two days in advance. Store at room temperature after wrapping in plastic.)

246.SPICED ICED TEA

Ready In: 20mins

INGREDIENTS

- 6cups of water
- 1tsp whole cloves
- 1inch piece cinnamon stick
- 3tea bags
- 1/2cup of sugar
- 3/4cup of orange juice
- 1tbsp lemon juice

DIRECTIONS

1. In a medium saucepan, mix the water, cinnamon stick, and cloves. up to a boil. Get rid of the heat.
2. Ten Mins should be allowed for the tea bags to steep in the spiced water.
3. Orange juice, lemon juice, and sugar should all be mixd in one more pan. up to a boil.
4. Pour tea into the combination of orange juice.
5. Serve chilled over ice.

247.SWEET CITRUS ICED TEA

- 14-1/2 cups of water, separated
- 10 tea bags
- 1-1/2 cups of sugar
- 2/3 cup of lemon juice
- 1/4 cup of thawed orange juice concentrate
- Ice cubes

Directions

1. Bring 4 cups of water to a gentle boil in a big pot. Get rid of the heat. Ten Mins should pass after adding tea bags. Throw away tea bags.
2. Into a big container, pour the tea. Add the remaining water, sugar, lemon juice, orange juice concentrate, and spices. Keep cold in the refrigerator. Serve chilled.

248.SUPER GREEN TEA SMOOTHIE

Ingredients:

- 1 Salada Green Tea bag
- 1 cup of spinach leaves
- 1 kiwi, peel off
- 1/4 avocado
- 1 banana, peel off, broken in chunks and refrigerate
- 1/2 tsp. of fresh ginger

Instructions:

1. Make green tea as directed on the package. Let to totally cool.
2. Blend the tea with the spinach, kiwi, avocado, banana, and fresh ginger.
3. Enjoy after blending till smooth!

249.STRAWBERRY-HIBISCUS GRANITA

Ingredients

- Makes 1 quart
- 2
- tbsp dried hibiscus flowers or 6 hibiscus tea bags
- 1
- sprig basil + leaves for garnish
- 1
- pound strawberries, hulled, quartered, + 1 1/2 cups of diced strawberries for garnish
- 1
- /2 cup of + 2 Tbsp. (or more) lighttagave syrup (nectar)

- 1
- tbsp (or more) fresh lime juice

Preparation

1. Using a small sauce pan, bring 112 cups of water to a boil. Add the basil sprig and hibiscus flower. After 20 Mins, turn off the heat, cover, and steep. Into a small basin, strain through a fine-mesh sieve. Hibiscus tea should be covered and chilled for at least one hour.

2. In the meantime, purée quartered strawberries in a blender until smooth. Place in a sizable bowl and top with tea, agave syrup, and 1 tbsp lime juice. Add extra agave and lime juice, as need, when seasoning.

3. Pour strawberry mixture into a 13x9x2" metal pan, and freeze for about 2 hours, or until top layer starts to set. Scrape the mixture with a fork to break up the refrigerate food into tiny bits. Scrape again after 30 Mins of freezing. Repeat for about 4 hours, or until the granita resembles fluffy shaved ice.

4. Distribute between the bowls. Split strawberries and basil leaves are used as a garnish.

250.STRAWBERRY, GRAPEFRUIT, AND CHAMOMILE BRUNCH PUNCH

Ingredients

- 10–12 servings
- Chamomile syrup:
- 3 cups of water
- 2½ cups of sugar
- 8 chamomile tea bags
- Punch:
- 4 cups of fresh grapefruit juice
- 1 pint fresh strawberries, hulled and split
- 3 cups of bourbon
- A few good dashes of bitters
- Ice cubes or an ice mold, for serving
- Fresh chamomile flowers, for garnish (non-compulsory)
- For the chamomile syrup:

Step

1. In a small pan over medium heat, mix the water and sugar. Stirring continuously until the sugar dissolves, bring to a simmer. Stir in the tea bags after turning off the heat in the pan. For 15 Mins, cover and allow to steep. Take out and throw away the tea bags. Refrigerate for at least one hour, or until cooled or at room temperature.
2. To make the punch:
3. Juice from one grapefruit and half of the strawberries should be blended together. Once smooth, blend. Mixture should be poured into a sizable punch bowl. Mix the bitters, bourbon, and chamomile syrup. Add ice and the remaining strawberry slices.
4. Pour the punch into glasses, top with fresh flowers, if available, and serve with a few ice cubes in the serving cups of.

251.SPICED WINE WITH DRIED FRUIT

Ingredients

- Makes 6 servings
- 2 chamomile tea bags
- 2 cups of boiling water
- 1 750-ml bottle Chenin Blanc or other semidry white wine
- 1/2 cup of sugar
- 1/3 cup of orange juice
- 1/4 cup of light rum
- 2 tbsp fresh lemon juice
- 1 tbsp raisins
- 1 tbsp chop up mixed dried fruit
- 1 bay leaf
- 1 cinnamon stick
- 1/8 tsp ground nutmeg

Step

1. In a large glass measuring cup of, put the tea bags. Pour over 2 cups of boiling water. Wait for four Mins. Throw away tea bags.
2. In a medium saucepan, mix the tea, wine, and remaining ingredients. Over medium heat, stir the wine mixture until the sugar dissolves. Just bring the mixture to a simmer. Get rid of the heat. For 20 Mins, cover and let steep.
3. Reheat wine on a low heat source (do not boil). Throw away the cinnamon stick and bay leaf. Wine, raisins, and dried fruit should be poured into cups of and served.

252.GINGERBREAD CHAI LATTE

Prep Time:5 Mins

Total Time:15 Mins

Ingredients

- 3 cups of Prairie Farms Milk
- 3 Tbsp sugar
- 1 chai tea bag
- 4 tsp ginger
- 2 cinnamon sticks
- 2 Gingerbread cookies, small

Instructions

1. In 1 cup of boiling water, steep the chai tea for 5 to 7 Mins.
2. Prairie Farms milk should be poured into mugs, along with sugar and ginger. Microwave for one minute. Never boil. Fill every cup of with chai tea.
3. With a cinnamon stick, stir. Serve right after after adding a gingerbread biscuit garnish.

253.PEANUT BUTTER AND HONEY CHAI LATTE

Prep time: 5 Mins

Cooking time: 15 Mins

Ingredients

- 3 cups of (750 mL) water
- 10 every whole cloves and black peppercorns
- 5 cardamom pods
- 2 cinnamon sticks
- 5 slices fresh ginger
- ½ cup of (125 mL) milk or soy milk
- 3 tbsp (45 mL) smooth peanut butter
- 2 tbsp (30 mL) honey or granulated sugar
- 3 bags black tea

Directions

1. In a medium saucepan, mix the water, ginger, and spices. Simmer for 10 Mins with a lid on and lower heat. Add honey, peanut butter, and milk and stir. Spend a few Mins simmering while stirring to completely melt the peanut butter. Add the tea bags, cover, and remove from heat after three Mins.
2. Tea should be strained into cups of using a large slotted spoon or strainer. Throw out the spices and tea bags.

254.EARL GREY TEA LATTE

INGREDIENTS

- 1 earl grey tea bag
- ¾ cup of boiling water
- ¾ cup of milk of choice*
- ½ to 1 tbsp vanilla syrup, depending on desired sweetness**
- sprinkle of cinnamon

INSTRUCTIONS

1. Boiling water is then added to the mug along with the tea bag. Let to steep for two to three Mins. Take away the tea bag.
2. In the meantime, put the milk in a little saucepan over medium heat. Up until just steaming, heat (do not let the milk boil). As an alternative, you can microwave the milk to reheat it. If desired, whisk the steaming milk until it is extremely foamy before adding it to the mug (or use a milk frother). Simply put, I like these lattes better without the foam.
3. Add the vanilla syrup after adding the milk to the mug. Sprinkle some cinnamon on top, then devour.

255.EASY MASALA CHAI (TEA) RECIPE – SPICED CHAI

Cooking Time: 20 MINS

total time: 20 MINS

INGREDIENTS

- 2 1/4 cups of (532 ml) filtered water
- 1 3-inch cinnamon stick, ceylon or cassia are both fine
- 3 whole cloves
- 4 green cardamom pods, cracked open and deseeded (I throw seeds & pods in)
- 3 black peppercorns
- 1/2 tsp fennel seeds, non-compulsory
- 1/2- inch (~4 g) fresh ginger, peel off and thinly split
- 3 black tea bags or sub 3 tsp loose leaf black tea, depending on brand, tea bags/leaves vary in strength (See Note 1)
- 1 cup of (8 oz) whole milk, or 2% reduced fat milk
- 4 tsp (20 g) turbinado cane sugar, or raw cane sugar

INSTRUCTIONS

1. A medium saucepan is heated on high. Add the water, ginger, fennel seeds (if used), cardamom pods, cloves, cinnamon stick, and black peppercorns. Observe Note 2 Add the tea bags or leaves once it has reveryed a boil.
2. Depending on how strong you want the tea and spices, reduce the heat to medium-low and simmer gently for 7–10 Mins. It will dim somewhat and change hue to a deep burgundy.
3. Stir in the milk and sugar. Put the heat on high (or allow the milk to come to a boil on its own, as I do on any given day). For a further five Mins, lower the heat to medium.

4. Depending on how "cooked" you prefer your milk, turn the heat up to high and let it come to a rolling boil for 1–2 Mins when you're ready to serve. (See Notation 3) If you'd want to enhance the flavor and make the chai creamier, aerate it with a ladle.
5. Pour through a strainer into cups of and, if desired, add extra sweetness.

256.SUPER GREEN TEA SMOOTHIE

TOTAL TIME: 5 Mins

Ingredients

- 1 cup of unsweetened almond milk
- ½ banana, peel off
- 1 cup of loosely packed fresh spinach leaves
- 1 cup of strawberries, hulled
- ¾ cup of ice
- 1 serving vanilla protein powder (1/2 to 1 scoop depending brand)
- ½ tsp matcha powder

Instructions

1. Blend together almond milk, banana, strawberries, spinach, ice, protein powder, and matcha powder.
2. For around 45 seconds, puree at high speed until the ice is perfectly smooth and not lumpy.

257. JASMINE BLOSSOM COCKTAIL

INGREDIENTS

- For the Jasmine Green Tea Gin:
- 350 ml gin
- 1 heaping tbsp Numi loose-leaf Jasmine Green tea
- For 1 Cocktail:
- 1 lychee (canned, syrup reserved)
- 2-3 tsp lychee syrup (chilled)
- ½ oz Jasmine Green Tea Gin
- Prosecco wine or other dry sparkling wine (chilled)
- 2 fresh raspberries
- 1 strip of lime peel

INSTRUCTIONS

1. Gin and tea leaves should be mixd in a glass container or mason jar, stirred, and left to infuse for 4 hours at room temperature. Discard tea leaves after straining.
2. Mix Jasmine Green Tea Gin with lychee syrup in a wine glass or champagne flute. Stir. Use lychee syrup instead of simp_e syrup when using fresh lychees. Add the raspberries and one lychee, cover with prosecco wine, and add a lime peel strip as a garnish.
3. Dispense and savor!

258.APPLE CIDER TEA

Cooking Time: 10 MINS

additional time: 5 MINS

total time: 15 MINS

INGREDIENTS

- 2 black tea bags
- 1 cup of unfiltered apple cider
- 1 cup of water
- 1 cinnamon stick
- lemon wedges for serving
- apple slices for garnish (non-compulsory)

INSTRUCTIONS

1. In a small pot, mix the apple cider, water, tea bags, and cinnamon stick.
2. Bring to a boil before simmering for 10 Mins or so.
3. Turn the heat off and give it a few Mins to cool. Pour tea into mugs after removing tea bags.
4. Warm drinks can be prepared by adding a thin slice of apple and fresh lemon juice to every mug.

259.LEMON GINGER TEA

PREP – 5 MINS

COOK – 5 MINS

REST TIME 10 MINS

TOTAL – 20 MINS

Ingredients

- 1 cup of water
- 1 heaping tbsp fresh grated ginger, start with ½ tbsp if you want it less spicy
- 1 large lemon, juiced
- Pinch turmeric, less than ¼ tsp
- Honey, to your taste
- Lemon slices, for garnish
- Non-compulsory Add Ons:
- 1 small cinnamon stick
- Fresh mint leaves

Instructions

1. Boil the water in a pot or tea kettle. Add the honey, honey, lemon juice, turmeric, and ginger (start with 1 tbsp of honey and add as you need).
2. Switch off the heat right away. Ten Mins should pass while the ginger tea steeps in the covered teapot.
3. Pour the ginger tea through a small mesh strainer that's been placed over your cup of. Add a lemon slice as a garnish.

260.HERBAL CHAMOMILE HEALTH TONIC

Active: 5 mins

Total: 20 mins

Servings: 4

Ingredients

- 4 cups of boiling water
- 6 bags chamomile tea
- 2 tsp grated fresh ginger
- 4 slices lemon
- 2-4 tsp honey
- 2 sprigs rosemary, lightly bruised

Directions

1. In a sizable heatproof bowl, mix the tea bags, honey, lemon, ginger, and rosemary. Boil the water. For 20 Mins, simmer while occasionally stirring. Press the tea bags to extract as much liquid as you can from the liquid as you strain it through a fine-mesh screen.

261.MATCHA GREEN TEA LATTE (HOT OR ICED)

Ingredients

- 1 tsp matcha green tea powder
- 2 tsp sugar
- 3 tbsp warm water
- 250ml cold milk or 300ml hot milk

Method

2. Put sugar and matcha powder in a mug:
3. Pour 2 tsp sugar and 1 tsp matcha green tea powder into a mug or cup of.
4. Combining with warm water:
5. To prevent lumps from forming, add 3 tsp warm water and whisk or mix with a spoon until it is a smooth, dark green paste.
6. adding milk
7. When the 250ml of milk is warm, pour it into the mug until it is almost full. If making an iced latte, use cold milk.
8. Blend well:
9. The paste and milk should be thoroughly blended and turned a light green color using a whisk.
10. Add a few sprinklings of matcha green tea powder to the top for decoration if you like. Then, garnish and serve. Or, for an iced latte that's extra chilly, add ice.

262.MINT ICED TEA

Prep: 5 min

Inactive: 2 hr 10 min

Cook: 5 min

Ingredients

- Deselect All
- 3 green tea bags
- 1 quart boiling water
- 1/4 cup of sugar
- 1/2 large lemon, split into 1/4-inch slices
- 1 bunch fresh mint, washed
- 2 cups of cold water

Directions

1. Tea should be steeped in boiling water for ten Mins. Tea should be poured into a pitcher for serving. Add sugar and lemon, then whisk in the mint while stirring and using the stems of the mint to help dissolve the sugar. Put the mint in the pitcher once the sugar has dissolved, then pour in 2 cups of cool water. Place in the fridge and let it get very cold. Before serving, remove the mint and serve it chilled.

263.PERFECT PEVERY ICED TEA

PREP TIME10 Mins

COOKING TIME40 Mins

TOTAL TIME50 Mins

Ingredients

- SIMPLE SYRUP
- 1 cup of organic cane sugar
- 1 cup of water
- 2 ripe peveryes (thinly split // + more for serving)
- TEA
- 2-3 Tbsp loose leaf black tea (3-4 tea bags // depending on how strong you prefer it)
- 8 cups of filtered water

Instructions

2. In a small saucepan, bring the sugar, water, and peveryes to a boil. After that, reduce the heat and whisk while crushing the peveryes to release their flavor.
3. Once the sugar has dissolved, cover the pan, turn the heat off, and let the mixture steep for 25–30 Mins.
4. Use a big pot or a tea maker to brew your tea in the interim. I use this IngenuiTEA loose leaf tea steeper. IMPORTANT: Try not to let it steep for more than 4-5 Mins as it will get bitter. Use less tea if you prefer it weaker or more tea if you prefer it stronger.
5. After brewing, take out the tea bags or drain the loose leaf tea into a pitcher. To chill, refrigerate.
6. Pour the resulting simple syrup into a bottle or other container over a fine mesh sieve to remove the peveryes. You can save the peveryes for later use, perhaps to top ice cream sundaes or oatmeal.

7. When ready to serve, either pour some simple syrup into the tea and stir, or pour all of the syrup into the tea and stir. I'd rather keep things apart. Tea should be served with fresh pevery slices over ice. The recipe makes approximately 10 servings as described (with ice and peveryes).

264.HONEY VANILLA ROOIBOS LATTE

Prep Time3 mins

Cooking Time5 mins

Total Time8 mins

Servings: 1

Ingredients

- 2 cups of unsweetened almond milk
- 1 sachet Pique Rooibos Vitality Elixir
- 1 tbsp honey + extra for serving
- 1/2 tsp vanilla bean paste
- 1/3 cup of frothed almond milk

Instructions

1. Almond milk is heated to a steaming point over a medium low heat. Honey, vanilla bean paste, and rooibos tea crystals are whisked in.
2. Pour into a big mug, then add frothed milk on top. On top, drizzle more honey. Enjoy it hot.

265.SPICED CHAI TEA LATTE

Cooking Time: 10 mins

Total Time: 10 mins

INGREDIENTS

- 4 cups of water
- 8 cardamom pods
- 4 whole cloves
- 1 tsp black peppercorns
- 4 whole star anise pods
- ½ tsp ground ginger
- 3 cinnamon sticks
- ¼ tsp ground nutmeg
- 4 darjeeling black tea bags
- 2 cups of milk
- ¼ cup of brown sugar, packed (use 2 tbsp if you like a spicer chai, and go up to a ⅓ of a cup of if you like a sweeter chai)

INSTRUCTIONS

1. Water, cardamom pods, cloves, peppercorns, anise pods, ginger, cinnamon sticks, and grated nutmeg should be brought to a boil in a medium pot. 5 Mins should pass after adding tea bags. After five more Mins of steeping, remove tea bags.
2. Brown sugar and milk are heated simultaneously over medium heat in a small sauce pan. Do not boil; scald. Blend till foamy with a whisk or an immersion blender. Give it one minute to cool.
3. Add milk after straining the tea. Have it warm or with ice!

266.HOMEMADE PUMPKIN CHAI LATTE

Prep Time: 5 mins

Cooking Time: 5 mins

Total Time: 10 Mins

INGREDIENTS

- Latte
- 1 tea bag of spiced chai (or decaf spiced chai rooibos)
- ½ cup of plain, unsweetened almond milk or milk of choice*
- 2 tbsp real pumpkin purée
- 1 tbsp real maple syrup or honey
- ¼ tsp vanilla extract
- ¼ tsp pumpkin spice blend (or ⅛ tsp ground cinnamon, ⅛ tsp ground ginger, dash of nutmeg, dash of cloves)
- Tiny dash salt

- ½ tsp arrowroot starch or cornstarch (non-compulsory, makes the latte super creamy)
- Non-compulsory garnishes: 1 cinnamon stick or star of anise, coconut whipped cream
- Non-compulsory coconut whipped cream
- 1 can (14 ounces) full fat coconut milk, chilled at least 10 hours (the coconut milk MUST be full fat and MUST be refrigerated for at least 10 hours. Put a mixing bowl in the freezer to chill while you're at it.)
- 1 tbsp maple syrup
- ½ tsp vanilla extract
- ⅛ tsp cinnamon

INSTRUCTIONS

1. Bring a quarter cup of water to a mild boil in a small saucepan. After adding the tea bag and removing the water from the boil, let it steep for 4 Mins. Squeeze out any excess water by pushing the tea bag against the pan's edge with the back of a spoon before removing it.
2. Salt, vanilla, pumpkin spice mix, maple syrup, almond milk, and pumpkin purée should all be added to the pan. Add the non-compulsory cornstarch or arrowroot starch after whisking. Once all the ingredients are mixd and the drink is smooth and creamy, pour the mixture into a stand blender and blend for about a minute. (You could also use an immersion blender, but my stand blender produced far superior results.)
3. The mixture should be poured back into the pan and warmed up slowly on the heat before being poured into a mug. Add whipped coconut cream over top at your discretion, and/or add a cinnamon stick or star anise as a garnish.
4. Making the coconut whipped cream requires: Get the mixing bowl and the coconut milk can from the refrigerator. Scoop the solid coconut cream from the coconut milk can into the bowl of cooled water (you can use the remaining coconut water in smoothies). The cream should be smooth and frothy after being beat with an electric hand mixer. Blend again briefly to incorporate after adding the cinnamon, vanilla essence, and maple syrup. Use the coconut cream right away, or cover and refrigerate it later (it will be soft at room temperature and more firm when cold).

267.BERRY HIBISCUS ICED TEA RECIPE

Prep Time15 mins

Cooking Time10 mins

Ingredients

- 6 Bags hibiscus tea or ¼ cup of loose leaf tea
- 1 cup of granulated sugar
- 2 cups of refrigerate berries
- 4 ½ cups of water
- 2 cups of ice

Instructions

1. creating the fruit syrup
2. 2 cups of refrigerate berries, 1 cup of granulated sugar, and half a cup of water should all be mixd in a small sauce pan.
3. Bring the berries to a boil in the medium-heated sauce pan. Once the heat is reduced, whisk the mixture until the sugar dissolves.
4. Turn off the heat and give the sauce pan some time to cool.
5. After the fruit syrup has cooled, liquefy it in a blender, making sure to get rid of any large bits.
6. To properly smooth out the syrup and get rid of all the seeds, pour the syrup through a sieve.
7. Prepare the tea
8. Bring 4 cups of water to a boil in a medium pot or tea kettle.
9. Add the tea bags and completely dunk them in the liquid. After removing the kettle from the heat, let the tea bags steep for ten to fifteen Mins.
10. Into a sizable serving pitcher, pour the tea. Mix in the berry syrup after adding it. 2 cups of ice should be added before placing the pitcher in the fridge to chill.
11. Berry hibiscus iced tea should be served in a large glass over ice and garnished with fresh berries or a lemon slice.

268. HOT TEA TODDY

Prep: 2 min

Inactive: 5 min

Cook: 5 min

Ingredients

- 1 Irish breakfast tea bag
- 1 1/2 ounces Scotch or brandy
- 1 heaping tbsp honey
- Boiling water
- 1/2 cinnamon stick
- 1 slice lemon
- Pinch ground nutmeg

Directions

1. Place the tea bag, Scotch, and honey in a coffee mug. Fill the mug with roughly 3/4 cup of hot water total. Lemon and cinnamon are added; steep for 5 Mins. Remove the cinnamon stick and tea bag.

Serve after a little nutmeg garnish.

269. CHOCOLATE PEPPERMINT TEA

INGREDIENTS

- 8ounces water
- 1peppermint tea bag

- 3tbsp chocolate syrup (I used Hershey's)
- 1(1 g) packet Splenda sugar substitute or (1 g) packet sugar, as need
- 1 -2tbsp non-dairy coffee creamer or 1 -2 tbsp cream
- whipped cream, to top
- chocolate syrup, to top
- crushed ice (non-compulsory)

DIRECTIONS

2. Heat the water in a mug in the microwave. Tea bag in hot water for a few Mins to steep Delete the tea bag.
3. Add the creamer, splenda, and chocolate syrup and stir.
4. If preferred, pour over broken ice in a large glass.
5. Add whipped cream and chocolate syrup over the top.

270.CHAI SPICE HOT CHOCOLATE

Cooking Time: 5 MINS

total time: 5 MINS

Ingredients

- 2 cups of oat milk
- 1/2 tsp ground cinnamon
- 1/2 tsp ground ginger
- 1/4 tsp ground all spice
- 1/4 tsp ground nutmeg
- Pinch of ground cardamom
- Pinch of ground cloves
- 1/2 tsp vanilla bean paste
- 3 tbsp maple syrup

- 4 tbsp cocoa powder
- Splash of hot water
- Whipped Cream
- 4 tbsp coconut cream from a tin of coconut milk
- 1 tbsp maple syrup

Instructions

1. Over medium heat, add the milk and maple syrup to a saucepan.
2. In a cup of, mix the spices and cocoa powder. Add a little boiling water, and stir until a paste forms.
3. Add this to the milk and well whisk. Let to warm on a low simmer.
4. When frothy and beaten, mix the coconut cream and maple syrup in a bowl using a hand-held mixer (or a whisk).
5. Fill mugs with the chai hot chocolate, top with whipped cream, and add more spices or cocoa powder for decoration.

271.VANILLA CHAI LATTE

Prep Time: 10 Mins

Cooking Time: 0 Mins

Ingredients

- 1 tsp Homemade Chai Spices
- 1 cup of water
- 1 bag black tea (or 1 tsp loose leaf black tea in a tea strainer)
- ½ cup of fresh 2% milk (or whole milk)*
- 1 tsp vanilla
- 1 tbsp pure maple syrup (or honey, agave, or simple syrup)

Instructions

1. Stir the chai spices, water, and tea bag in a small saucepan over medium-high heat until the mixture comes to a boil. Once it has boiled, turn off the heat and give it a minute to cool. Then pour into one or two mugs after passing through a fine mesh strainer (one for a large latte and two for small).
2. Clean out the saucepan. Add the milk, maple syrup, and vanilla. Use a thermometer to check the milk's temperature; it should be heated with a few little bubbles appearing on the outside, but not simmering. For the best foam, you need the precise temperature (but you can approximate if you don't have a thermometer).
3. To foam the milk, use a hand frother, a whisk, or a French press. (A popular way is the French press: add the hot milk and vigorously press until frothy, roughly 100 times for 2% milk or about 1 minute; use 50 times for full milk.) To allow the foam to set, rest it for around 30 seconds. If this is your first time frothing, go visit How to Froth Milk.
4. Divide the milk and froth among the mugs (or into 1 mug). Add more chai spices after you've served.

272.ORANGE SPICE TEA MIX

INGREDIENTS

- 2cups of instant Tang orange drink (must be Tang, not Kool Aid)
- 1cup of instant tea, mix sweetened and lemon flavor
- 1 1/2cups of sugar
- 2tsp cinnamon
- 1tsp ground allspice
- 1tsp ground cloves

DIRECTIONS

1. Mix all ingredients in a bowl. Use an airtight container for storage.
2. How to use: To a cup of or mug of boiling water, add approximately 2 heaping tbsp. Stirring vigorously

273.BLUEBERRY-LEMON ICED TEA

Serves 4

Ready in 20mins

Prep time 10mins

Cooking time 10mins

Ingredients

- 8 oz fresh blueberries or refrigerate (1 ½ cups of)
- 3 tbsp fresh lemon juice (from 1 lemon)
- 4 cups of water
- 6 tea bags (black or green tea)
- 2 Tbsp honey

Steps

1. Over medium heat, bring blueberries and lemon juice to a boil in a medium saucepan. Blueberries should be soft after 5 Mins of cooking, stirring occasionally. Remove from the heat and pour into a bowl through a fine wire-mesh strainer. Juice can be squeezed out with the use of a spoon. Throw away the remaining blueberry flesh in the strainer.
2. Clean the pan, add water, bring to a boil, add tea bags, and let stand for five Mins. Take out and throw away the tea bags. Add honey and blueberry juice combination, and stir. Pour the mixture into a pitcher, cover it, and chill until serving time. Serve chilled.

274.CITRUS ICED TEA

Prep:15 mins

Ingredients

- 6 ordinary tea bags
- 2 tbsp caster sugar
- 10 sprigs mint
- 300ml fresh orange juice
- juice 1 lime
- 1/2 split orange, mint leaves and ice to serve

Method

1. STEP 1 Prepare the tea with the sugar and 1.2 liters of water. Infuse the kettle with mint for 10 Mins. Drain, then cool.
2. STEP 2 Pour the mixture into a jug, add the juices, and whisk to mix. Garnish with orange slices, mint, and lots of ice.

275. CARAMEL VANILLA CHAI LATTE

Prep Time 2 Mins

Cooking Time 15 Mins

Total Time 17 Mins

Servings 2

Ingredients

- 2 cups of water
- 2 peppercorns
- 3 whole cloves
- ⅛ tsp nutmeg
- ¼ tsp ground cardamom
- ¼ tsp fresh grated ginger
- 1 cinnamon stick
- 2 rooibos tea bags
- 1-2 tbsp caramel sauce or syrup
- 1 tsp vanilla extract
- ½ cup of milk

Instructions

1. In a small saucepan, mix water, peppercorns, cloves, cardamom, ginger, nutmeg, and a cinnamon stick. Bring to a boil and continue to boil for five Mins minimum.
2. After removing the heat, add the tea bags to the water. For 5 to 6 Mins, steep.
3. Add vanilla and caramel sauce and stir.
4. Stir the milk into the tea after heating it in the microwave for 15 seconds on medium.
5. If desired, add more caramel sauce and whipped cream over top.
6. Serve right away.

276.RASPBERRY ICED TEA

Prep: 10 min. + chilling

Ingredients

- 8-1/4 cups of water, separated
- 2/3 cup of sugar
- 5 tea bags
- 3 to 4 cups of fresh or refrigerate unsweetened raspberries

Directions

1. Bring 4 cups of water to a boil in a big pot. Add sugar and mix until it dissolves. Add tea bags after removing from the heat. For 5-8 Mins, steep. Throw away tea bags. Add 4 cups of water.
2. Bring the raspberries and remaining water to a boil in a separate pan. Lower heat; allow to simmer for 3 Mins, covered. Remove pulp, then discard it. juice from a raspberry to the tea mixture. Pour over ice in cold glasses.

277.CUCUMBER MINT GREEN ICED TEA

Prep:20 mins

Cook:3 hrs 30 mins

Total:3 hrs 50 mins

Servings:9 servings

Ingredients

- 8 cups of brewed Japanese green tea
- 1/2 cup of peel off, seeded, and pureed cucumber
- 1/4 cup of mint leaves, lightly chop up and muddled
- 1/4 cup of freshly squeezed lime juice, or lemon juice
- Simple syrup, or another tea sweetener, non-compulsory
- Cucumber slices, for garnish, non-compulsory
- Fresh mint leaves, for garnish, non-compulsory

Steps to Make It

1. assemble the components.
2. Mix the green tea, cucumber puree, mint, and lime juice in a sizable pitcher or bowl. If desired, add sweetness as need.
3. For many hours, refrigerate the mixture with the pitcher covered.
4. If desired, strain the mint and cucumber and throw them away.
5. To every glass, add ice. If desired, add some cucumber slices as a garnish to the rim. Not simply on the rim of the glass, cucumber also looks good inside. If desired, add mint leaves to the tea.

278.MASALA CHAI LATTE

Active Time: 10 mins

Total Time: 25 mins

Servings: 4

Ingredients

- 8 green cardamom pods
- 5 whole cloves
- 2 (3-inch) cinnamon sticks
- 1 tsp black peppercorns
- ½ tsp fennel seeds
- 3 cups of water
- 1 (2-inch) piece fresh ginger, peel off and thinly split (about 2 tbsp)
- 3 tbsp granulated sugar
- 4 individual-size black tea bags
- 1 whole nutmeg, grated (about 1/2 tsp)
- 1 ¼ cups of whole milk

Directions

1. Cardamom pods can be cracked open using the bottom of a mug or small bowl. Over medium heat, warm a medium saucepan. Add the cardamom pods that have been cracked, along with the cloves, cinnamon, peppercorns, and fennel. Cook, stirring frequently, for 2 to 3 Mins, or until the mixture is fragrant.
2. Add water and ginger to the mixture in the pan and heat to a boil. Medium-low heat should be used; cover the pot and simmer uncovered for five Mins. Get rid of the heat. Add sugar and stir until it dissolves. Add the tea bags, then gently whisk. Add nutmeg lightly, cover, and soak for 10 Mins.
3. Add milk to the pan's mixture. Pour into a medium-sized heatproof dish or carafe through a fine mesh sieve; discard sediments. Serve over ice or return to pan and cook over medium, untouched, for 2 Mins, or until milk is well warmed.

279.LEMON THYME GREEN TEA

Prep/Total Time: 20 min.

Ingredients

- 2 quarts water
- 8 green tea bags
- 12 fresh lemon thyme sprigs or 8 fresh thyme sprigs + 1/2 tsp grated lemon zest
- 1/4 cup of honey
- 3 tbsp lemon juice
- Sugar, non-compulsory
- Shop RecipePowered by Chicory

Directions

1. Bring water to a boil in a big pot, then turn off the heat. Tea bags and lemon thyme sprigs should be added; steep covered for 3 Mins. Tea bags should be discarded after 3 Mins of covered steeping. strain tea. Lemon juice and honey should be added; mix until honey is dissolved. If using, stir in sugar. Serve right away.

280.PEPPERMINT TEA LATTE

Prep time 10 mins

Total time 10 mins

Ingredients

- 1½ cups of Plain, Unsweetened Almond Milk*
- 1 Peppermint Tea Bag OR 1 drop Peppermint Essential Oil
- 2 tsp Maple Syrup

Instructions

2. Almond milk should be heated until it is hot and boiling, either on the stove or in a microwave-safe container. (between two and three and five Mins in the microwave)
3. If using a tea bag, soak it in the milk, covered, for five to seven Mins. Take remove the tea bag after drinking it, then whisk in the maple syrup. If you're using it, mix the peppermint oil with the maple syrup.
4. Add liquid to a blender at high speed. 15 to 20 seconds should be blended to achieve foamy liquid. The liquid will become more foamy the more you mix it.
5. Put to mug and start enjoying right away.

6. Notes *You can use almond milk that has been sweetened or flavored with vanilla! Before adding the maple syrup, you should taste the beverage to make sure it isn't already very sweet.

281.SPICED COCONUT CHAI TEA

Prep Time: 5 Mins

Cooking Time: 10 Mins

Total Time: 15 Mins

Ingredients

- 1 tbsp fresh ginger, chop up
- 1 tsp fennel seeds
- 8 green cardamom pods
- 3 clove buds
- 10 black whole peppercorns
- 3 tbsp coconut sugar*
- 1 cinnamon quill* (around 7cm / 2.76 inches)
- 2 tbsp loose black tea leaves
- 2 cups of / 500ml coconut milk (not from a can)

Instructions

1. Start by using a mortar and pestle to grind the fresh ginger.

2. After the ginger has finished cooking, add the remaining spices (aside from the cinnamon quill) and crush them as shown above, being careful to break the walls of all the cardamom pods.
3. 2 cups of/500 ml of water, sugar, and spices—including the cinnamon quill—should be added to a small, deep saucepan and brought to a boil.
4. Add a spoonful of cold water to the pot after the food has boiled.
5. Add the coconut milk slowly while adding the black tea, and cook for 5-7 Mins.
6. After straining, pour the tea.

282.GINGER-TURMERIC HERBAL TEA

Prep Time: 5 mins

Cooking Time: 15 mins

Total Time: 20 mins

Servings: 2

Ingredients

- 2 cups of water
- ½ tsp ground turmeric
- ½ tsp chop up fresh ginger
- ½ tsp ground cinnamon
- 1 tbsp honey
- 1 lemon wedge

Directions

1. Add turmeric, ginger, and cinnamon to a small pot of boiling water. Medium-low heat should be used to simmer for 10 Mins.

2. Tea should be strained into a tall glass; add honey and a wedge of lemon before serving.

283.MAPLE APPLE CIDER TEA LATTE

Ingredients

- 1/2 cup of water
- 3 Stash Maple Apple Cider tea bags
- 1 cup of milk
- Ground cinnamon
- Milk Frother

Directions

1. Pour 1/2 cup of boiling water into a glass.
2. 3 Stash Maple Apple Cider tea bags should be steeped for 3 Mins before being removed.
3. Froth 1 cup of the milk of your choosing.
4. Then, fill the glass with frothed milk. A little mixing will do.
5. Cinnamon powder should be sprinkled on top, then done!

284.CHAI-SPICED APPLE CIDER RECIPE

Prep:4 mins

Cook:20 mins

Total:24 mins

Servings:4 servings

Ingredients

- 4 whole allspice corns
- 4 whole cloves
- 3 cardamom pods
- 2 tsp cinnamon chips
- 1/2 tsp dried ginger root
- 1/2 vanilla bean pod (seeds removed)
- 1/2 small apple (such as Honeycrisp, Jonagold, or McIntosh)
- 4 cups of apple cider (fresh-pressed is preferable)
- 2 tbsp assam loose leaf black tea
- 1/2 cup of almond milk (if desired, you can omit this or use other dairy alternatives)

Steps to Make It

1. assemble the components.
2. Crush the ginger, cinnamon, allspice, cloves, and cardamom pods very lightly in a mortar and pestle.

3. Add the apple cider, vanilla bean, crushed spices, and apple slices to a small saucepan.

4. After bringing the mixture to a boil, turn off the burner.
5. For 10 Mins, cover and let steep.
6. Bring the spiced cider back to a boil before turning off the heat.
7. Add the almond milk and tea. For 4 Mins, cover and let steep.
8. Mix thoroughly, then pour into a teapot.
9. Dispense and savor!

285.MAPLE PECAN LATTE RECIPE

Prep:10 mins

Cook:2 mins

Total:12 mins

Serving:1 serving

Ingredients

- For the Maple Pecan Syrup:
- 1/4 cup of maple syrup
- 1/4 cup of pecan butter
- 2 tbsp brown sugar, packed
- 1/2 tbsp unsalted butter

- 1/3 cup of heavy cream
- 1 tsp pure vanilla extract
- For the Latte:
- 1 (1-ounce) shot espresso
- 2 tbsp maple pecan syrup
- 1/2 cup of steamed milk
- Dollop store-bought or homemade whipped cream, for garnish
- Chop up toasted pecans, for garnish

Steps to Make I

1. Construct the maple-pecan syrup.
2. assemble the components.
3. Over medium-high heat, mix the maple syrup, pecan butter, brown sugar, and butter in a small pot. Around 2 Mins of cooking and stirring is required to completely dissolve the sugar.
4. After taking the syrup off the heat, mix in the vanilla extract and heavy cream. Place aside and allow to fully cool. There will be enough syrup for 8 lattes.
5. Produce the latte
6. assemble the components.
7. In a mug, stir together the espresso and 2 tbsp of the maple pecan syrup.
8. Steamed milk should be added, followed by whipped cream and toasted pecans on top.

286.HOT ORANGE SPICE CIDER

INGREDIENTS

- 1cup of fresh orange juice
- 5whole cloves
- 6cups of apple cider
- 6bags apple cinnamon spice tea
- 1slice orange rind, for garnish (non-compulsory)

DIRECTIONS

1. All ingredients should be mixd in a big pot.
2. Cook for ten Mins.
3. Tea bags and entire cloves should be strained out.
4. Pour hot cider into thermos bottles that have been heated.
5. Serve warm.
6. Add orange rind as a garnish.
7. Double the recipe and cook it in your crockpot on high for two to three hours for a party service.
8. To make it simple to retrieve the cloves and tea bags without straining, tie them in a piece of cheesecloth before placing them in the crockpot.

287.STRAWBERRY LEMONADE SWEET TEA

INGREDIENTS

- 8 tea bags (I use a black tea, but feel free to use a green or mint tea)
- 8 cups of water + 4 cups of water
- 1 8 oz can refrigerate lemonade concentrate
- 1 8 oz can refrigerate strawberry concentrate or strawberry daiquiri
- 6 cups of ice
- 2 cups of fresh strawberries, chop up
- 1 lemon, split

DIRECTIONS

1. Start by brewing the tea. Bring 8 cups of water to a rolling boil. Tea bags must be added and brewed according to the directions (usually around 3-5 Mins). Add the

lemonade and strawberry concentrate after removing the tea bags. Mix everything together until it has "melted" completely.

2. After the concentrate has melted, add 4 cups of water and 6 glasses of ice. You may want to add more water if the tea is overly sweet. But be aware that doing so can make the beverage less strong. Fill a large pitcher or beverage dispenser with the contents. Once you are ready to serve, keep cold.

3. As a garnish, lemons and fresh strawberries are utilized.

288.CARAMEL APPLE CIDER TEA

Prep time:10 Mins

Cooking Time:10 Mins

Ingredients

- For the caramel sauce:
- ½ cup of granulated sugar
- 3 tbsp salted butter, slice into 6 pieces
- ¼ cup of heavy cream
- ½ tsp vanilla extract
- For the whipped cream:
- ½ cup of heavy cream
- 2 tbsp granulated sugar
- ½ tsp vanilla extract
- For the cider tea:
- 2 cups of apple cider
- 2 tbsp Tea Forté Harvest Apple Spice Loose Leaf Tea
- Non-compulsory garnishes:
- Ground cinnamon
- Cinnamon sticks

Directions

1. Making the caramel sauce involves adding the sugar to a medium pot and stirring continuously with a wooden spoon over medium-high heat. It will start to clump up and then transform into a liquid that is amber in color. Stir the butter in as soon as the sugar is completely dissolved. Although it will bubble or foam, keep mixing until it is thoroughly mixed. Slowly incorporate the heavy cream while stirring. After another minute of stirring, the mixture will begin to bubble and foam once more, but it will soon subside. Next turn off the heat and mix in the vanilla extract in your pan. Pour into an other bowl and leave to cool. Note: Rather than preparing your own caramel sauce, you can use your favorite brand from the store to save time.
2. Whip the cream as follows: In a dish, mix the heavy cream, sugar, and vanilla extract. Whip rapidly until stiff peaks appear, then set aside.
3. For the cider tea, steep the loose leaf tea for two Mins in two cups of hot cider. For this, you can either use a dedicated tea kettle or a medium saucepan. Remove the tea leaves from the steeping solution and discard them.
4. Make the beverages: Divide the hot apple cider tea equally between two mugs (these Joey Mugs are a nice option) and add a little amount of caramel sauce to every. Add freshly prepared whipped cream, crushed cinnamon, and additional caramel on top. Enjoy with a cinnamon stick as a garnish!

289.CHAI-SPICED APPLE CIDER RECIPE

Prep:4 mins

Cook:20 mins

Total:24 mins

Servings:4 servings

Ingredients

- 4 whole allspice corns
- 4 whole cloves
- 3 cardamom pods
- 2 tsp cinnamon chips
- 1/2 tsp dried ginger root
- 1/2 vanilla bean pod (seeds removed)
- 1/2 small apple (such as Honeycrisp, Jonagold, or McIntosh)
- 4 cups of apple cider (fresh-pressed is preferable)
- 2 tbsp assam loose leaf black tea
- 1/2 cup of almond milk (if desired, you can omit this or use other dairy alternatives)

Steps to Make It

1. assemble the components.

2. Crush the ginger, cinnamon, allspice, cloves, and cardamom pods very lightly in a mortar and pestle.

3. Add the apple cider, vanilla bean, crushed spices, and apple slices to a small saucepan.

4. After bringing the mixture to a boil, turn off the burner.

5. For 10 Mins, cover and let steep.

6. Bring the spiced cider back to a boil before turning off the heat.

7. Add the almond milk and tea. For 4 Mins, cover and let steep.

8. Mix thoroughly, then pour into a teapot.

9. Dispense and savor!

290.MAPLE CHAI TEA LATTE RECIPE

Prep Time5 mins

Total Time5 mins

Servings: 1

Ingredients

- 1 1/2 cups of milk regular, almond, coconut etc.
- 1 -2 chai tea bags 2 for stronger flavor
- 1/2 tsp pure vanilla extract
- 1 tbsp pure maple syrup
- Non-compulsory: ground cinnamon nutmeg or allspice

Instructions

1. Milk can be heated in a microwave or on the stovetop until it is steaming but not boiling.
2. After adding heating milk to the tea bags in the mug, steep for three to five Mins.
3. remove the tea bag (s).
4. Add maple syrup and vanilla and stir.
5. Pour hot into a mug and enjoy.

6. Add a little sprinkle of ground cinnamon, nutmeg, or allspice, if desired.

291.ALMOND MILK CHAI TEA

15 min prep

2 servings

Ingredients

- 2 cups of almond milk
- 3 chai tea bags
- ½ tsp vanilla extract
- 1 tsp cinnamon
- ½ tsp ground cloves

Directions

1. Almond milk is warmed in a sauce pan. Get rid of the heat. Tea bags should be added, covered, and steeped for 5-7 Mins.
2. Remove tea bags, then stir in ground cloves, cinnamon, and vanilla.
3. Serve after pouring into tea glasses. Alternatively allow to cool and then pour over ice.

292.BLUEBERRY-LEMON ICED TEA RECIPE

Prep Time: 5 mins

Cooking Time: 10 mins

Additional Time: 1 hrs 5 mins

Total Time: 1 hrs 20 mins

Ingredients

- 1 (16-oz.) package refrigerate blueberries
- 1/2 cup of fresh lemon juice
- 4 cups of water
- 3 family-size tea bags
- 3/4 cup of sugar

Directions

1. In a large saucepan over medium heat, bring 1/2 cup of fresh lemon juice and 1 (16-oz.) package refrigerate blueberries to a boil. Cook for 5 Mins while occasionally stirring. Remove from heat, then pour into a bowl through a fine wire-mesh strainer, pressing juice out with the back of a spoon. Throw away solids. Clean the saucepan.
2. In the same saucepan, bring 4 cups of water to a boil. Add 3 family-size tea bags, and let steep for 5 Mins. Take out and throw away the tea bags. Mixture of blueberry juice and 3/4 cup of sugar are added. Pour into a pitcher; secure the lid, and chill for an hour. Serve chilled.

293.RASPBERRY-LIME ICED TEA

INGREDIENTS

- 1 1/2cups of slightly defrosted refrigerate raspberries
- 6tbsp sugar
- 1/4cup of lime juice
- 4cups of ice-brewed black tea or 4 cups of ice-brewed green tea

DIRECTIONS

1. In a food processor, mix all the ingredients (apart from the tea) and process until extremely smooth.
2. Pass through a cheesecloth or fine sieve to filter.
3. Blend into tea.
4. Some individuals favor more sugar. Serve chilled.

294.VANILLA ALMOND CHAI LATTE

PREP TIME: 15 MINS

COOKING TIME: 5 MINS

TOTAL TIME: 20 MINS

Ingredients

- 1 cup of fine-ground dark roast coffee
- 1 tbsp + 1 tsp ground cinnamon, separated
- 2 tsp ground cardamom
- 1 1/2 tsp ground ginger
- 1 tsp ground allspice
- 1 tsp peel off and grated fresh ginger

- 1/4 tsp black pepper
- 1/8 tsp ground cloves
- Large pinch of salt
- 4 cups of cold water
- 1 tbsp granulated sugar
- 1 1/2 cups of vanilla almond milk or regular milk
- 1/2 cup of sweetened condensed milk

Instructions

1. Coffee, 1 tbsp cinnamon, cardamom, ground ginger, allspice, freshly grated ginger, pepper, cloves, and salt should all be blended in a medium basin. Pour into a drip coffee maker's filter. Fill the machine with cold water, then brew. (OR, add the ingredients in a 48-ounce French press coffee maker with cold water; cover the machine while the plunger is extended. Press the plunger after letting the mixture steep for 4 to 5 Mins.
2. In the meantime, mix the remaining 1 tsp of cinnamon and sugar in a small bowl.
3. Over medium-high heat, add milk to a medium saucepan. 5 Mins of continuous whisking will produce foam that is fully warmed.
4. In a sizable mixing bowl (ideally one with a lip/pour spout), pour sweetened condensed milk. Pour brewed coffee on top and stir to mix. Put mixture into every coffee cup of.
5. The foam on top of the milk in the pot can be removed with a spoon. Every mug should have a small amount of milk in it, followed by froth. Add some cinnamon-sugar mixture as a garnish.

295.HOT APPLE CIDER WITH GINGER

Ingredients

- 1 lemon, scrubbed, + slices for serving
- 4 cups of apple cider
- 1 cinnamon stick

- 8 whole cloves
- 2 inches fresh ginger, peel off and thinly split

Directions

1. Peel the lemon zest in long strips using a vegetable peeler (avoiding the white pith). Lemon juice, 2 tsp, squeezed.

2. Cider, cloves, ginger, cinnamon, and lemon zest should all be mixd in a medium pot. Over high heat, bring to a boil, lower the heat to a simmer, cover, and cook for 10 Mins. Withdraw from heat and stand for 10 Mins. Add lemon juice, sieve, and then remove any particles. Lemon slices should be served warm.

296.BLUEBERRY LAVENDER LEMONADE

Ingredients

- 2 cups of water
- 1 package (16 ounces) blueberries
- 1/4 cup of granulated sugar
- 1 tbsp dried lavender flowers
- 1 cup of lemon juice
- 2 tbsp Splenda sweetener
- Cold water

Directions

1. Add 4 cups of ice to a 1-gallon pitcher and reserve. Bring two cups of water to a rolling boil in a medium saucepan. To the pan, add the lavender, sugar, and blueberries. Boil for approximately 5 Mins, or until all of the sugar has dissolved and the blueberries have popped.
2. Discard the remaining blueberry mixture after straining it over the ice-filled pitcher. Splenda and lemon juice should be added to the pitcher. Add cold water until it is about full. Mix well.

297.VANILLA PEVERY TEA

Ingredients

- 1 gallon of fresh brewed tea
- For the Vanilla Pevery Simple Syrup
- 2 cups of Tate+Lyle® Organic Pure Cane Sugar
- 2 cups of water
- 1 vanilla bean, split
- 4-5 fresh peveryes, peel off and split

Instructions

1. The ingredients for the Vanilla Pevery Simple Syrup are mixd and simmered in a small sauce pan. Simmer it until the liquid has been slice in half.
2. Remove the peveryes and vanilla bean from the syrup.
3. One gallon of freshly brewed tea should be mixed with syrup until it reveryes the required sweetness.

298.VANILLA MATCHA LATTE (SERVED HOT)

prep time: 1 MINUTE

Cooking Time: 3 MINS

additional time: 1 MINUTE

total time: 5 MINS

Ingredients

- 1 tsp matcha powder
- 2 ounces filtered water
- 1-2 tsp vanilla syrup
- 6 ounces 2% milk

Instructions

1. Water should be heated to 175 degrees Fahrenheit. While you wait, steam milk in the microwave or on the stovetop until it reveryes 150°F.
2. Pour matcha into a cup of and, if preferred, use a sifter to remove any lumps. 2 ounces of water should then be added. Until it's smooth, whisk it or use a handheld aerator (frother). Add vanilla syrup and mix as need.
3. When the milk is warm, froth it until a glossy layer of microfoam has formed on top. Pour the remaining froth on top of the vanilla matcha latte before adding the milk.

299.LEMON & GINGER TEA

Prep:5 mins

Ingredients

- 1 lemon
- 2cm piece root ginger, lightly split
- honey as need

Method

1. Lemon must be slice in half. Slice the remaining half, then squeeze the juice from one. Together with the split ginger, distribute the lemon juice and slices across 2 mugs.

2. Boil the water in the mugs, then let it steep for three Mins or until it is cold enough to drink from. If desired, add honey to sweeten.

300.VANILLA CHAI TEA LATTE RECIPE (ICED)

Prep Time: 10 Mins

Cooking Time: 15 Mins

Total Time: 25 Mins

Ingredients

- 1 pc chai tea bag
- 1 cup of boiling water
- 1 tbsp sugar
- ¼ tsp vanilla extract
- 2 tbsps Half and Half

Instructions

1. Add boiling water to a cup of with a tea bag inside. Remove the bag after letting it steep for approximately 3 to 5 Mins. In a saucepan, mix sugar, extract, and half and half. Mixture heating to a medium temperature The mixture is prepared when little bubbles start to appear. Pour into the cup of the mixture from the pan. Place ice in a large glass after pouring everything inside. You may now serve your vanilla chai tea latte to your customers!

Printed in Great Britain
by Amazon